Cook from the heart!
Andrea

Kitchen Alchemy
Encore

Andrea Tzadik

Outskirts Press, Inc.
http://www.outskirtspress.com

Paperback ISBN: 978-1-9772-0097-6
Hardback ISBN: 978-1-9772-0098-3

Edited and Designed by Sandy Smith © 2018 All Rights Reserved – Used with Permission.
Cover & Interior Photos© 2018 Andrea Tzadik, Sandy Smith, Loong Kong;
Cover Photos © 2011 Terry Greenberger (peppers, onions, lettuces)

Outskirts Press and the "OP" logo are trademarks belonging to Outskirts Press, Inc.

PRINTED IN THE UNITED STATES OF AMERICA

INTRODUCTION

My first cookbook, Kitchen Alchemy, was published in 2012. It was a joint effort with my dear friend, accomplished cook and editor, Sandy Smith. It was a large collection of tried and true family recipes, with just a few pictures. People who use it say they love it for its clear instructions and delicious results!

Friends know that I am always trying new recipes and revamping old favorites for one reason or another. Over and over, I have been asked for a second cookbook, and many people have requested lots of pictures. This new book, Kitchen Alchemy Encore, has pictures of most recipes and in some cases documents the process when it is unusual. The photos were taken by family and friends as opportunities presented themselves. Come to dinner at my house? You might be asked to take photos! Make one of these recipes at home or go to the farmer's market? Send me a photo! I offer my heartfelt thanks to all these willing photographers. It has been a labor of love all around!

Many recipes in this book have been adapted to be as healthy as possible. Having a large family with many food sensitivities and allergies, it can at times be challenging even for the most experienced cook. I have provided notes in many recipes on how to make them gluten free, dairy free and/or vegetarian to accommodate those food issues.

Since childhood, cooking has been a wonderful way for me to express my creativity, love of exceptional foods and tastes – and to feed the people I love. It has been great fun to write down the recipes and share them. Few things give me more satisfaction than having someone tell me they made one of my recipes and it was has become a family favorite at *their* house!

The profits from sales of this new book will go to charitable causes. Hopefully it will make a difference to those in need.

Bon Appetite!

Andrea

COMPLETE RECIPE LISTING BY CATEGORY

COMPLETE RECIPE LISTING BY CATEGORY

Main Dishes

Side Dishes

COMPLETE RECIPE LISTING BY CATEGORY

Desserts & Other Sweets

See Complete Alphabetical Recipe Listing, page 109

Sandy and Andrea

Appetizers, Dips
& Snacks

BAKED EGGS WITH SPINACH AND MUSHROOMS

This is a kind of green Shakshuka - a breakfast or brunch treat that is healthy, delicious and comforting. You can make the spinach mixture ahead and do the eggs just before serving.... because who wants cold poached eggs?

INGREDIENTS

3 lbs. fresh spinach, washed and dried (Swiss chard also works well)
¼ cup extra virgin olive oil
1 medium onion, diced
8 oz. mushrooms, sliced
6 large eggs
1 teaspoon salt
Freshly ground black pepper, to taste
Turkish Salad or Moroccan Matbucha (Matbucha recipe p. 17)

INSTRUCTIONS

1. Preheat oven to 350°F.
2. Heat oil in a large skillet and add onion. Sauté until transparent. Add mushrooms and continue to sauté for about 2 minutes more.
3. Add spinach by the handful, and cook just until wilted.
4. Transfer spinach mixture to a 9x13" baking dish.
5. Make six indentations in the spinach mixture. Put a teaspoon of Turkish Salad or Matbucha into the bottom of the indentation, followed by a carefully cracked egg (do not break the yolk). Sprinkle with coarse salt and black pepper.
6. Bake for 15-30 minutes, until eggs are set and cooked to your preferred doneness.
7. Serve immediately.

Ready for the oven

Oops - Someone couldn't wait!

CHOPPED LIVER PÂTÈ

Better than anything that comes out of a jar; this chopped liver pâté can be enjoyed on crackers, bread or with raw vegetables.

INGREDIENTS

1 chicken liver
1 onion, diced
1 egg, hardboiled and peeled
¼ cup olive oil
¼ teaspoon McCormick brand Montreal Steak Seasoning
Salt and fresh ground pepper to taste

INSTRUCTIONS

1. Heat the oil in a saucepan and add the diced onions.
2. Cook onions until they have browned.
3. Sprinkle the steak seasoning on the chicken liver.
4. Add the liver to the saucepan.
5. Cook the liver until no blood can be seen when it is cut into, about 5 minutes.
6. Add the liver, onions and hardboiled egg to a food processor and chop fine.
7. Add salt and pepper to taste.
8. Process all the ingredients until they are pureed.
9. Serve in a decorative bowl and add ground pepper on top.

CHICKPEA SAMBUSAK
Chickpea Turnovers

Sambusak has long been a favorite in our household. They can be pulled out of the freezer 10 minutes before guests are due to arrive. Simply reheat in a 400° toaster oven until heated through. This traditional Jewish-Iraqi recipe was handed down from my father-in-law. I bake them instead of deep frying to make them healthier. Serve with Moroccan Matbucha (p. 17) or Tahini Dip (p. 16).

INGREDIENTS

Filling

2 cups dried garbanzo beans (chick peas)
  (soaked overnight in cold water)
1 whole clove garlic
6 onions, diced
⅓ cup extra virgin olive oil
4 tablespoons ground cumin
2 teaspoons salt, divided
2 teaspoons harissa

Dough

3 cups unbleached white flour
4 cups whole wheat pastry flour
  (or white whole wheat flour)
½ cup extra virgin olive oil
2 eggs
1 teaspoon salt
1 package yeast
warm water, as directed

INSTRUCTIONS

Filling
1. Boil soaked and drained beans in enough water to cover, with 1 teaspoon salt and the garlic clove, for about 1½-2 hours, until soft.
2. Sauté the onions in olive oil until golden brown.
3. While the onions are sautéing, process the cooked and drained beans in a food processor until the mixture has the consistency of cornmeal.
4. Add spices and 1 teaspoon salt to cooked onions and combine with the beans.
5. Refrigerate overnight, or for a minimum of 2 hours.

Dough
1. Dissolve yeast in ¼ cup of warm water and 1 teaspoon of sugar to proof.
2. Put all the other *dough* ingredients into a bowl and add the yeast mixture.
3. Add more warm water to the dough while working it. The dough should be firm, not sticky. Start with 1 cup of warm water and add more as needed.
4. Place dough in an oiled bowl, cover with a dish towel and let rise for 1-1½ hours.

Assembly and Baking
1. Preheat oven to 350°.
2. Roll out ¼ of the dough until it is about ⅛ of an inch thick.
3. Cut circles in the dough with a cookie cutter or jelly glass.
4. Place 1 heaping teaspoon of the filling into the middle of each dough circle and pinch closed to make half moon shapes.
5. Bake at 350° on cookie sheets, about 15–20 min until golden brown.
6. Repeat the process with the rest of the dough and filling.
7. When thoroughly cooled, pack in plastic freezer bags and freeze until needed.

CHICKPEA SAMBUSAK
Assembly Process

Filling and dough ready for assembly

Circle of dough flattened for wrapping

Ready for the oven

Served with Moroccan Matbucha

EGGPLANT PUFF PASTRY BOREKAS

The original recipe for this came from my neighbor in Israel, Benny Finger. Benny taught young men to be chefs in the Israeli Army. He made this using fried eggplant and chopped up liver. I use grilled eggplants and no liver for a healthier vegetarian version of his creation.

INGREDIENTS

1 medium eggplant, cut in ½" slices
½ cup extra virgin olive oil
1 medium onion, diced
1 clove garlic, crushed
1 red bell pepper, diced
½ cup green olives, chopped
½ cup fresh flat leaf parsley, chopped
1 teaspoon dried oregano
2 eggs, beaten (for filling)
1 egg, beaten (for brushing on top crust)
Frozen puff pastry dough, thawed
  (Pepperidge Farm or your favorite brand)

INSTRUCTIONS

1. Slice eggplant, place on cookie sheet and brush with olive oil on both sides. Place under the broiler until browned. Repeat on the other side.
2. Sauté onion in olive oil until transparent. Add bell pepper and sauté until fragrant. Add garlic and cook for 1 minute more. Remove from heat.
3. Cube the eggplant slices and add to onions and peppers.
4. Quickly add olives, parsley, oregano and eggs. Mix well.
5. Thaw four pieces of puff pastry dough. Roll out to form two long rectangles (for top and bottom), the length of your cookie sheet.
6. Lay one rectangle on the oiled cookie sheet; this is the bottom crust. Cover with filling, leaving a border of ½" all the way around.
7. Gently fold second rectangle in half lengthwise, and snip the folded edge about every inch, snipping at a slight angle. This may be done with a sharp knife or kitchen scissors. When unfolded, it will provide a center row of V shaped vents for the top layer of pastry.
8. Lay the vented pastry over the filling and seal the sides well by crimping with a fork or by pinching with your fingers. Brush top crust with beaten egg.
9. Bake at 400°F for 20-30 minutes, until golden brown. Slice and serve.

EGGPLANT PUFF PASTRY BOREKAS
Assembly

Filling centered, with margins for sealing

Top crust with vents and pinched edges

GUACAMOLE WITH GREEN PEAS

This recipe was given to me by my friend and amazing cook, Sandy Smith. It adds fiber and bumps classic guacamole up a notch!!!

INGREDIENTS

2 ripe avocados
1 cup green peas, cooked until just tender
and cooled before adding
2 tablespoons fresh lime juice
   (lemon juice as a second choice)
Pinch of salt
⅓ cup diced red or sweet onion (raw)
½ cup quartered cherry tomatoes
   (or more, to taste)
1-2 cloves garlic, crushed through a press

INSTRUCTIONS

1. Cook green peas in boiling water or in the microwave until just tender. Rinse with cold water, drain and allow to cool.
2. Mash avocado with lime juice, garlic and salt.
3. Mash cooled peas and add to avocado mixture.
4. Mix in onions and tomatoes.
5. Serve immediately or chill in airtight container. To minimize oxidation, place plastic wrap directly on top of guacamole with no air gaps, then seal container. Keeps fresh for about 2 days in the refrigerator.

Note: If you want a very smooth mixture, use a food processor before adding the onions and tomatoes. I prefer a chunkier version, and mash the avocados and peas with a spoon.

Inspired by a recipe in *Nutrition Action Health Letter*, March 2016

HUMUS

For years I made humus from canned Garbanzo beans, and everyone liked it. However, once I chanced on this method of making it, it blew me out of the water! By starting with dried beans and adding two types of garlic, cooked and raw, there is a whole new complexity of flavor. It only lasts 7 days in the refrigerator because it has no preservatives, but you can freeze it for months.

INGREDIENTS

½ cup dried garbanzo beans, soaked overnight
   in cold water
3 whole cloves garlic, unpeeled
1 clove garlic, peeled, trimmed and crushed
   (or more, to taste)
½ cup tahini paste
2 Tablespoons extra virgin olive oil
½ teaspoon salt
Juice of one lemon

INSTRUCTIONS

1. Place soaked and drained garbanzo beans in a medium saucepan with cold water ½ inch over beans. Bring to a boil and skim off the white foam. Reduce heat and bring to a simmer. Add unpeeled garlic, cover the pot and cook until beans are tender, one to two hours.
2. Scoop the cooked beans out of the pot with a slotted spoon, <u>reserving the cooking liquid</u>. Place beans in a food processor with other ingredients, including the garlic cloves cooked with the beans (squeeze garlic cloves out of their skins).
3. Add ½ cup of cooking liquid and process for 2 minutes. Taste and adjust seasonings (it may need more salt, garlic or lemon juice). Add more cooking liquid if needed to make the consistency a little more runny than typical humus, as it will firm up in the refrigerator.

Makes about two cups.

TAHINI DIP
Sesame Dip

Tahini dip is another traditional Israeli dish that is served with many sandwiches in Israel. The amount of water used in this recipe will depend on the desired thickness of the spread.

INGREDIENTS

1 cup sesame seed paste (tahini)
1 tablespoon extra virgin olive oil
¼ cup lemon juice
1 teaspoon salt
¼ - ½ cup water
1 – 2 cloves garlic, crushed
1 bunch fresh parsley

INSTRUCTIONS

1. Pour 1 tablespoon of olive oil into your one cup measure. Swirl it around to coat all inner surfaces. Pour or spoon sesame seed paste from the jar into the oiled measuring cup. The oil will keep the paste from sticking to the cup.
2. Place the sesame seed paste, lemon juice, salt and garlic into a food processor.
3. Blend the ingredients until they form a lumpy dry mass.
4. Slowly add in the water while continuing to blend the mixture.
5. Continue to blend the mixture until it becomes the thickness of sour cream.
6. Add in the parsley and then continue to blend until the parsley is chopped into small pieces.
7. Taste the Tahini dip and add more of any ingredients as desired.
8. Refrigerate for storage, but bring back to room temperature to serve.

MAZAL'S MOROCCAN MATBUCHA
Spicy tomato and pepper dip

My sister-in-law Mazal is the queen of Middle Eastern salads. I make a large batch of her Matbucha when tomatoes and peppers are in season and freeze it in serving portions. It's wonderful with Chickpea Sambusak!

INGREDIENTS

10 lbs. ripe tomatoes, diced
3 red bell peppers
3 light green Hungarian peppers
10 hot peppers (your choice of how hot)
1 whole head of garlic, cloves crushed through a press
½ cup extra virgin olive oil
2 teaspoons salt
1-2 teaspoons sugar (optional)

INSTRUCTIONS

1. Roast red bell and Hungarian peppers under the broiler until the skin is charred. Remove from oven, drop peppers into a paper bag and allow to sit until cool enough to handle. The charred skin will peel off easily after steaming in the bag. Dice the peppers.
2. Seed the hot peppers (use gloves) and dice.
3. In a large stock pot, sauté garlic quickly, add remaining ingredients and bring to a boil.
4. Reduce heat to a simmer and cook until the consistency of jam. This will take several hours.
5. Taste and adjust salt and spiciness.
6. If a spicier version is desired, add hot red pepper flakes as needed.
7. Cool and divide into small containers or freezer bags. Keep in the freezer for up to a year.

MOROCCAN BASTILLA
Spiced chicken pie

This has all the flavor of the classic Moroccan dish, but is easier for the home cook. The process is much like the Eggplant Boreka recipe, but the filling is very different.

INGREDIENTS

Filling
1 lb ground chicken or turkey
½ teaspoon salt (omit if using Kosher meat)
1 onion, diced
1 teaspoon t'bit seasoning or Ras El Hanout (Moroccan seasoning)
1 teaspoon ground cinnamon
3 tablespoons extra virgin olive oil
½ cup fresh parsley, finely chopped
2 eggs, beaten

Crust
Frozen puff pastry, thawed (Pepperidge Farm or your favorite brand)
1 egg, beaten
Powdered sugar for dusting top (optional)

INSTRUCTIONS

Filling
1. Sauté onions until lightly browned. Add meat and cook until browned.
2. Add remaining ingredients, mixing in the beaten eggs last. Set aside in the refrigerator until just before baking.

Crust
3. Thaw four pieces of puff pastry dough. Roll out to form two long rectangles (for top and bottom), the length of your cookie sheet.
4. Lay one rectangle on the oiled cookie sheet; this is the bottom crust. Cover with filling, leaving a border of ½" all the way around.
5. Gently fold second rectangle in half lengthwise, and snip the folded edge about every inch, snipping at a slight angle. This may be done with a sharp knife or kitchen scissors. When unfolded, it will provide a center row of V shaped vents for the top layer of pastry.
6. Lay the vented pastry over the filling and seal the sides well by crimping with a fork or by pinching with your fingers. Brush top crust with beaten egg.
7. Repeat steps 3-6 for second log.
8. Bake at 400°F for 20-30 minutes, until golden brown. Dust lightly with powdered sugar when it is still warm, but not straight out of the oven.

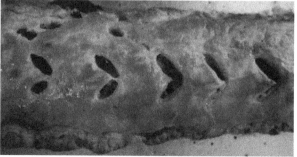

MOROCCAN BASTILLA
Process

Ready for the oven   *Baked golden brown*

SOFT PRETZELS

This is a fun recipe to make with kids - who will want to eat them hot out of the oven! You can also let them cool thoroughly and then freeze them in airtight bags for reheating later.

INGREDIENTS

1½ cups lukewarm water
1 packet active dry yeast (2¼ teaspoons)
1 teaspoon salt
1 tablespoon sugar
½ cup extra virgin olive oil
3¾ to 4¼ cups all-purpose flour, plus a little more for dusting board or table top **OR**
      a mixture of all-purpose and white whole wheat flours
1 large egg, lightly beaten
Coarse salt for topping (or cinnamon sugar)

INSTRUCTIONS

1. Preheat oven to 425°F. Prepare cookie sheet with parchment paper or a silicone baking mat.
2. In a large mixing bowl, dissolve yeast in warm water. Stir for about 1 minute and then add sugar and salt, continuing to stir until lumps have dissolved. Add olive oil and blend in.
3. Add 1 cup of flour at a time for the first 3 cups, mixing with a wooden spoon until dough is thick. Gradually add ¾ cup or more flour until dough is no longer sticky. It will be ready to knead when you can poke it and it bounces back.
4. Scoop the dough out of the bowl onto your floured surface. Knead for about 3 minutes and form a smooth ball.
5. Cut the ball into sections of about ⅓ cup each, using a sharp knife. This can be larger or smaller, depending on how you like your pretzels.
6. Roll each portion of dough with your hands into a long rope of consistent thickness, about 18 - 22 inches long. First make a circle with the rope, and then twist into a pretzel shape.
7. In a large pot, bring 9 cups of water to a boil and whisk in ½ cup of baking soda. Using a large slotted spatula, dip a pretzel into the boiling water for 20 to 30 seconds (longer will make it taste metallic). The pretzel will float and be easy to scoop back out. Shake gently to remove water. Place onto prepared baking sheet. Repeat with remaining pretzels. This additional step is for the texture of the finished product.
8. In a small bowl, beat the egg and pour into a shallow bowl. Dunk the shaped pretzel into the egg wash on both sides. Place on baking sheet and sprinkle with salt or cinnamon sugar.
9. Bake for 10 minutes or until browned. Watch closely that they do not burn.
10. Cool and serve warm or at room temperature. Store in an airtight container for up to 3 days, or freeze for up to 2 months. If frozen, reheat at 350°F for 20 minutes.
11. The prepared dough can be refrigerated for up to one day or frozen in an airtight container for 2-3 months. Thaw frozen dough in the refrigerator overnight. Refrigerated dough can be shaped into pretzels while still cold, but allow some extra time for the pretzels to puff up before the baking soda bath and baking.

SOFT PRETZELS

Maya kneads the dough

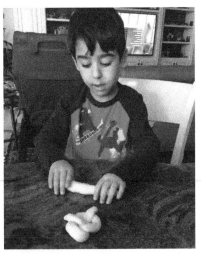

Jordan rolls and forms pretzels

Baking soda boiling bath

Ready for toppings

Noah (and Kat) add cinnamon sugar

Jonah adds coarse salt

SHAKSHUKA FRITTATA

Spicy baked eggs with peppers and tomatoes

My daughter-in-law Avital loves Shakshuka and asked me to make it for her son's birthday party. I felt it would be daunting to make traditional Shakshuka for so many people, so I tried this version, which can be made ahead. It was a big success – there wasn't a scrap left!

INGREDIENTS

2 onions, diced
4 red and/or yellow bell peppers, diced
¼ cup extra virgin olive oil
1 cup Moroccan Matbucha salad (see recipe, p. 17, or purchase jar at Middle Eastern store)
14 eggs, lightly beaten
4 ripe red tomatoes, sliced

INSTRUCTIONS

1. Preheat oven to 350°F.
2. Prepare 9x12 inch Pyrex baking dish with cooking oil spray. Set aside.
3. Sauté onions in EVOO until lightly browned.
4. Add diced peppers and cook for 1 minute.
5. Mix in Matbucha and then beaten eggs.
6. Pour into the oiled Pyrex baking dish. Top with sliced tomatoes.
7. Bake at 350°F for 30 to 45 minutes, or until eggs are set.

Salads

HEALTHY COLESLAW

No mayonnaise in this take on a classic side salad. Without mayo, the slaw is light and fresh… appropriately named the "healthy coleslaw." This slaw is also a terrific sandwich ingredient that goes with a variety of meats and cheeses.

INGREDIENTS

Salad

1 large head cabbage, shredded <u>OR</u>
   2 small heads, one red and one green
2 carrots, shredded

Dressing

1 teaspoon salt
⅓ cup white vinegar
⅓ cup extra virgin olive oil
1 teaspoon sugar

INSTRUCTIONS

1. After shredding the cabbage and carrots, place in a large mixing bowl to allow extra room for tossing.
2. Mix the ingredients for the *dressing* in a small bowl.
3. Pour the dressing over the vegetables and toss.
4. Cover and refrigerate for 1 – 2 hours or more before serving.
5. Keeps in the refrigerator for up to 1 week.

INDIAN CHICKPEAS

I first tried this dish for a birthday party for my first Yoga teacher, Chris Stein. Marilyn Clair, another of Chris's students, said she knew how to make it and sent me the recipe. It is great to serve as a side salad or as a main dish for vegetarians.

INGREDIENTS

4 teaspoons extra virgin olive oil
1 cup diced onions
½ teaspoon turmeric
½ teaspoon cumin
½ teaspoon coriander
¼ teaspoon cayenne pepper
2 15-oz. cans chickpeas, drained and rinsed
  OR 1 cup dried, soaked and boiled
4 teaspoons fresh lemon juice
¼ teaspoon salt
Black pepper to taste
2 tablespoons cilantro, chopped
  (use flat leaf parsley if preferred)

INSTRUCTIONS

1. Heat a large sauté pan over medium heat. When hot, add the oil and allow to heat but not smoke, add the onion and sauté until deeply colored, about 6 to 8 minutes, stirring periodically.
2. Add the turmeric, cumin, coriander and cayenne pepper and continue to sauté until the spices are aromatic and a bit toasted, about 3 minutes.
3. Add the chickpeas, lemon juice, salt and pepper and cook for another 5 minutes to blend the flavors.
4. Remove from heat and cool. Store in the refrigerator, or mix in the fresh cilantro or parsley and serve immediately.

MARINATED LENTILS

This recipe originally came from the Inn of the Golden Ox on Cape Cod, about 1980. My friend, Sandy Smith, got it from the innkeepers. The taste and texture are fresh and light, partly due to the hulling of the lentils. If you can find hulled lentils, this is much easier!

INGREDIENTS

1 lb. lentils
½ cup minced red onion
½ cup chopped fresh flat leaf parsley
15 grinds black pepper
Salt to taste (lentils will absorb, so make salty)
¼ cup fresh squeezed lemon juice
½ cup grape seed oil (olive oil is too heavy)

INSTRUCTIONS

1. Soak the lentils in hot water for 1 hour. Rub lentils between palms under warm water, down to the yellow bean. Discard skins. This process is time consuming but worth it. It will take several changes of water to complete.
2. Drain, set in cold water in a medium saucepan, sprinkle with salt and put on medium flame. When steam forms, but before water boils, test lentils for "not raw" texture. Drain, rinse with cold water, drain again.
3. Make marinade. Toss drained lentils with marinade and refrigerate. Allow to marinate for at least a couple of hours before serving.
4. Keeps about 2 weeks.

MOROCCAN CARROT SALAD

This salad offers a symphony of flavors – sweet carrots, tangy lemon garlic dressing, bright cilantro, a jolt of chili from the harissa... Addictive!

INGREDIENTS

Salad   2-3 lbs. carrots, peeled and trimmed
2 tablespoons extra virgin olive oil
¼ cup fresh cilantro or parsley,
    chopped fine

Dressing   ¼ cup extra virgin olive oil
3-4 tablespoons fresh squeezed
    lemon juice
2-4 cloves garlic, crushed through a press
1-2 teaspoons ground cumin
1 teaspoon sweet paprika
½ teaspoon salt
½ teaspoon Harissa or hot red pepper
    flakes (or more, to taste)

INSTRUCTIONS

1. Preheat oven to 400°F.
2. Peel carrots and trim ends.
3. Place whole carrots in a 9 x 13" baking dish. Drizzle with 2 tablespoons olive oil, and roll carrots around to coat.
4. Roast carrots for about ½ hour, shaking/turning them after 15 minutes. Test for tenderness.
5. Allow to cool until they are comfortable to handle, and slice into ¼" thick rounds.
6. Mix the dressing ingredients with the cilantro in a bowl.
7. Cover the carrots with the mixture and then toss.
8. Refrigerate and serve either cold or room temperature.

PAMELA'S SHALLOT VINAIGRETTE

My sister-in-law Pamela, inspired by my first cookbook, created her own garlic-free version of my French Vinaigrette.

INGREDIENTS

2 medium shallots
2 tablespoons Dijon mustard
1 teaspoon Kosher salt
⅓ cup champagne vinegar
1 cup extra virgin olive oil
1 cup avocado oil

INSTRUCTIONS

1. Place all ingredients in a blender, and blend until smooth.
2. Store in a glass jar or bottle in the refrigerator.

QUINOA SALAD

This is a versatile and healthy salad. You can add any vegetables you like for variety. I've added cherry tomatoes, red bell peppers, sugar snap peas etc. It's also great as written.

INGREDIENTS

½ cup quinoa, soaked overnight in cold water
½ cup dried black beans, soaked overnight in cold water
1 clove garlic, whole
½ cup Kalamata olives, pitted and sliced
½ cup dried cranberries
¼ cup chopped chives
Grated zest of one lemon
½ cup chestnuts or other nuts, chopped
1 tablespoon extra virgin olive oil
1 tablespoon avocado oil
½ cup purple basil, torn (optional)
1 ripe avocado, sliced and added last

INSTRUCTIONS

1. Boil the soaked quinoa in plenty of water for 15 minutes, then drain well and allow to cool.
2. Boil the soaked beans with the garlic clove until beans are tender, then drain and allow to cool. Discard garlic clove or use for something else.
3. Mix all ingredients except the basil and avocado.
4. Just before serving, add basil and fresh avocado, mixing in gently.

SCARLET RUNNER BEAN SALAD

This combination of beans and herbs reminds me of Italy! Fava beans also work well.

INGREDIENTS

1½ cups fresh scarlet runner beans
   (if using dried beans, soak overnight in cold water)
1 clove fresh garlic with skin left on
1 clove fresh garlic, crushed
½ cup fresh basil, chopped just before using
½ cup fresh mint, chopped just before using
½ teaspoon sea salt
¼ cup extra virgin olive oil

INSTRUCTIONS

1. Remove fresh beans from the pods (discard pods).
2. Bring beans to a boil in plenty of water with the whole clove of unpeeled garlic. Lower heat and simmer until beans are tender.
3. Drain cooked beans and discard whole garlic clove. While beans are still hot, mix in salt, crushed garlic and olive oil.
4. When cooled to room temperature, add chopped herbs and serve.
5. Best served room temperature, but can be stored in refrigerator for up to one week.

VIETNAMESE CABBAGE SALAD

This is a very popular salad in Vietnam. The dish can have shredded chicken, and/or crushed peanuts or almonds added to make it a main dish.

INGREDIENTS

Salad
4 cups Napa or Savoy cabbage, shredded
1 bunch green onions, sliced
1 cup carrots, shredded
2 Persian cucumbers, julienned
¼ cup mint leaves, minced
¼ cup cilantro, minced (optional)

Dressing
1 teaspoon agave nectar (or sugar)
3 tablespoons rice vinegar
4 tablespoons fresh lime juice
1 tablespoon Vietnamese fish sauce
1 clove garlic, minced
1 teaspoon Vietnamese hot sauce (to taste)
3 tablespoons toasted sesame oil

INSTRUCTIONS

1. Finely shred the cabbage.
2. Add the carrots, cucumbers, onion, mint and cilantro.
3. Combine the *dressing* ingredients in a bowl and whisk together.
4. Pour the dressing over the salad and toss.
5. Serve at room temperature. Refrigerate leftovers.

Soups

BLACK BEAN SOUP WITH STEALTH VEGETABLES

This is a favorite with the grandkids. They love the beans but don't know about the chard.

INGREDIENTS

1½ cups dried black beans,
  soaked overnight
2 garlic cloves, unpeeled
2 medium onions, diced
4 garlic cloves, peeled and crushed
¼ cup extra virgin olive oil
6 carrots, diced
3 stalks celery, diced
2-4 zucchini, diced
1 bunch Swiss chard, chopped in food
  processor with:
  1 bunch flat leaf parsley
2 teaspoons chili powder
2 teaspoons ground cumin
1 teaspoon sea salt
32 ounces chicken or vegetable broth

INSTRUCTIONS

1. Place soaked beans in a large soup pot and cover with water. Bring to a boil and skim off white foam.
2. Add whole unpeeled garlic cloves and simmer until beans are tender.
3. Once the beans are tender, scoop out the garlic cloves and remove husks. Return peeled cloves to the pot.
4. Sauté chopped onions in olive oil until transparent. Add crushed garlic, chili powder, cumin and salt. Sauté for another minute or two and add to the soup pot.
5. Add the remaining ingredients and cook on low heat for 30 minutes or until diced vegetables are tender.
6. Allow to cool and then refrigerate. This soup is best the second day.

CHICKPEA AND CHARD SOUP WITH SWEET POTATO
Vegan

This hearty vegetable soup can be served as a first or main course. The smoked paprika really adds depth of flavor.

INGREDIENTS

1½ cups dried chickpeas, soaked overnight
¼ cup extra virgin olive oil
4 whole cloves garlic, peeled
1 onion, chopped
2 teaspoons ground cumin
1 teaspoon honey or agave syrup
1 teaspoon ground coriander
1 teaspoon smoked paprika
¼ teaspoon cayenne pepper, or more to taste
3 cups diced chard
1 bunch Italian flat leaf parsley
2-4 medium sweet potatoes, diced
4 carrots, diced
3 turnips, diced
1 box vegetable broth (32 oz.)

INSTRUCTIONS

1. Drain soaked chickpeas, and then cook with garlic cloves in plenty of fresh water until tender. Drain.
2. Sauté onion in olive oil until lightly browned. Mix in spices and add onion mixture to soup pot with cooked chickpeas.
3. Chop chard and parsley in a food processor.
4. Add remaining ingredients, bring to a boil and reduce to a simmer for 20-30 minutes, until vegetables are tender.

COCONUT CHICKEN SOUP
Tom Kha Gai

This is one of our family's favorite soups when we eat at Thai restaurants. I had to learn to make it at home to insure I could accommodate all my family members' food allergies. It's a winner!

INGREDIENTS

I.   4 chicken leg quarters (leg and thigh with skin and bones)
      8 cups water
      6 cloves garlic, peeled and trimmed
      3 stalks fresh lemongrass, tough outer layers removed, then smashed with a rolling pin
      5 tablespoons fish sauce
      1 inch piece of fresh ginger, peeled and cut in half

II.   Zest of one lime
      ¼ cup fresh lime juice
      2 onions, diced
      1½ cups chopped cabbage (optional) or 2 turnips or small daikon radishes, diced
      14 ounce can coconut milk
      1 teaspoon sugar
      8 ounces of mushrooms, sliced, or 4 carrots sliced thin
      Chili oil or Sriracha sauce, to taste
      2 kaffir lime leaves, if available

INSTRUCTIONS

1. Make broth with ingredients in section I. Bring to a boil in a large pot, then lower the heat and simmer for 1 hour. Remove chicken parts, but continue to simmer the broth while you remove the meat and skin from the bones. Discard skin, refrigerate meat, and return bones to the pot. Simmer for another 1-4 hours. Cool overnight - in refrigerator or outside (if outside is chilly).
2. The next morning, discard bones, ginger and lemongrass.
3. Shred the chicken and return to the pot.
4. Add ingredients in section II and bring to a boil. Lower heat and simmer 15-20 minutes.
5. Serve with lime wedges and fresh cilantro.

For a vegetarian version, omit chicken, use vegetable broth and replace fish sauce with soy sauce.

FAVA BEAN SOUP

My family loves fava beans and in the spring, when they come into season and show up at the farmer's market, we relish their rich taste. This soup is very flavorful, green and light.

INGREDIENTS

2 pounds fresh fava bean pods,
  beans removed and pods discarded
4 medium carrots, diced
1 head spring garlic, chopped
1 onion, chopped
1 turnip, diced
1 teaspoon chicken or vegetable bouillon
  (*Better Than Bouillon* brand)
2 cups water
1 teaspoon salt
Cayenne pepper to taste
1 bunch fresh basil - 1 cup of leaves,
  washed and loosely packed
¼ cup extra virgin olive oil

INSTRUCTIONS

1. Remove fava beans from the pods and set aside.
2. Sauté diced carrots, onions, garlic and turnip in olive oil until soft, and set aside.
3. In a soup pot, dissolve chicken bouillon paste in 2 cups of hot water, just off the boil.
4. Bring broth to a boil and add fava beans. Lower to a simmer and cook 15 minutes.
5. Add salt and cayenne pepper to taste.
6. Add basil leaves and puree until smooth.
7. Stir sautéed vegetables into puree and heat to serving temperature.

IRAQI BUTTERNUT SQUASH AND MEATBALL SOUP

This Iraqi classic can also be made with beets or pumpkin instead of the butternut squash.

INGREDIENTS

Meatballs
1½ lbs. ground turkey or beef
1 onion, diced
1 bunch fresh flat leaf parsley, minced
1 teaspoon salt
1 teaspoon ground cinnamon
1 teaspoon ground cumin
1 teaspoon paprika
1 dash cayenne pepper, to taste

Broth and Vegetables
1 onion, chopped
1 teaspoon salt
1 teaspoon ground cinnamon
1 teaspoon ground cumin
1 teaspoon cayenne pepper
1 teaspoon sweet paprika
1 teaspoon turmeric
1 teaspoon chicken *Better Than Bouillon*
¼ cup fresh squeezed lemon juice
2-4 tablespoons sugar
2-4 tablespoons extra virgin olive oil
1 small can tomato paste
¼ cup goji berries or raisins
2 lbs. butternut squash or beets in 1 inch cubes
6 cups water

INSTRUCTIONS

1. In a large mixing bowl, combine all the *meatball* ingredients and mix well. Once mixed, set the bowl aside.
2. In a soup pot, sauté the chopped onion in the olive oil until the onion becomes transparent.
3. Add the rest of the *Broth* ingredients (excluding the butternut squash), including enough water to make a good sized batch.
4. Bring the broth to a boil and then lower the heat to a simmer.
5. While the broth simmers, form round meatballs about 1 inch in diameter.
6. Add the meatballs to the broth and simmer on low heat for 1 hour.
7. Add the cubed butternut squash and cook for another 20 minutes.
8. Serve as is or over rice, as desired.

LENTIL SOUP WITH AN IRAQI TWIST

Iraqi food makes use of cumin and garlic as spices in many typical dishes. I also added the butternut squash, which is a favorite Iraqi ingredient and offers a pleasing contrast to the lentils.

INGREDIENTS

2 turkey necks or other bones (beef marrow bones or chicken bones)
6 cups water
1 cup lentils, soaked overnight in cold water
1 onion, diced
¼ cup extra virgin olive oil
1 cup chard or spinach, chopped in a food processor
1 bunch Italian flat-leaf parsley, chopped in a food processor
2 cups butternut squash, cubed
1 teaspoon ground cumin
4 cloves garlic, 2 whole and 2 minced
1 teaspoon *Better than Bouillon*
¼ teaspoon cayenne pepper, or more to taste

INSTRUCTIONS

1. In a large soup pot, place turkey necks and 2 whole garlic cloves in the water and bring to a boil. Reduce to a simmer and let cook for 3-5 hours.
2. Cool overnight in the refrigerator (or outside if it is cold enough).
3. Heat broth, adding rinsed lentils, greens and bouillon. Cook for 1 hour.
4. Sauté onion in olive oil until browned. Add minced garlic and cook until fragrant (about 1 minute). Add cumin and cayenne.
5. Add onion mixture to the broth.
6. Add cubed squash and simmer for 30 minutes more.
7. Serve immediately, or reheat later.

MOROCCAN CHICKPEA VEGETABLE SOUP
Vegan

I first put this together for a yoga party that included a number of vegans. It's a keeper!

INGREDIENTS

Chickpeas	1 cup dried chickpeas, soaked overnight and boiled until tender
Vegetables and Fruit	2 onions, diced
	6 garlic cloves, minced
	1 medium butternut squash, peeled, seeded and cubed (½ inch pieces)
	1 pound delicata squash, seeded and sliced ½ inch thick (no need to peel)
	3 large carrots, sliced ½ inch thick
	3 stalks celery, sliced ½ inch thick
	1 firm, ripe plantain, sliced ½ inch thick
	1 2" piece fresh ginger, peeled and left whole
Herbs	1 bunch cilantro, divided
	1 bunch Swiss chard (or other dark leafy green such as spinach or kale)
	1 bunch flat leaf parsley
Spices	¼ - 1 teaspoon cayenne pepper, to taste
	1 teaspoon cinnamon
	1 - 2 teaspoons ground cumin
	1 - 2 teaspoons turmeric
	1 teaspoon salt
Liquids and Oil	1 box vegetable broth (32 ounce box)
	1 can unsweetened coconut milk (13.5 ounce can or more, to taste)
	Juice of 1 lemon
	1 teaspoon sugar or agave syrup
	6 tablespoons extra virgin olive oil

INSTRUCTIONS

1. In a large soup pot, sauté onions in olive oil until transparent. Stir in spices and garlic.
2. Wash herbs well. Set aside about ¼ of the cilantro for garnishing finished soup. Chop remainder of cilantro along with the Swiss chard and parsley in a food processor.
3. Add vegetable broth, coconut milk and all remaining ingredients to the pot.
4. Bring to a boil and then reduce heat. Simmer for 30-45 minutes, until vegetables are tender.
5. Serve as a soup or ladle over rice or couscous. It's even better the second day!

VIETNAMESE CHICKEN ASPARAGUS SOUP
Minh's Soup

When we lived in Iowa, I worked as an English teacher for Vietnamese students who had come to the states after the war. These students became close friends with my family and were responsible for teaching Ron to use chop sticks before he knew how to use a fork. One student gave us this soup recipe. It was everyone's favorite soup in our household, and we called it "Minh's soup." It is still a favorite, all these years later.

INGREDIENTS

Stock
6 chicken thighs, bone-in, skin on
12 cups water
1 slice fresh ginger root, 3 inches long
6 whole garlic cloves
2 onions, diced
2 turnips, peeled and chopped
1 tablespoon chicken *Better Than Bouillon*
2-4 tablespoons Vietnamese fish sauce
1 teaspoon salt
½ teaspoon freshly ground black pepper
2 tablespoons toasted sesame oil
4 cloves garlic, crushed through a press

Add-ins: Vegetables and Noodles
1 bunch green onions, sliced
4 heads baby bok choy, sliced
1 bunch fresh asparagus
3 eggs, beaten
2 cups sugar snap peas, ½ inch slices
2 cups cooked rice noodles (optional)
Fresh cilantro and Asian basil for garnish

INSTRUCTIONS

1. Place the chicken and water in a stock pot over high heat and bring to a boil.
2. Skim excess chicken fat off the top of the broth and then reduce the heat to a simmer.
3. Sauté the crushed garlic in the sesame oil until fragrant and add to stock.
4. Add the rest of the *stock* ingredients and then cover.
5. Simmer the stock for 2-4 hours. At the one hour point, scoop out chicken pieces, remove and discard skin, shred chicken meat, return bones to the broth. Place chicken meat in the refrigerator. Continue simmering the broth.
6. Just before serving the soup, carefully remove the bones. Add the shredded chicken, asparagus, sugar snap peas and the bok choy. Cook on a simmer for another 5 minutes.
7. Add the beaten eggs and stir.
8. Place the green onions in each serving bowl before spooning out hot soup into them. Serve hot.
9. If preferred, serve the soup with cooked rice noodles and garnish each bowl with fresh herbs. Fill each bowl with the desired amount of rice noodles (may be more or less than a total of 2 cups).
10. The stock will keep in the refrigerator for up to one week, but make sure to keep add-ins separate until you are ready to serve the soup. For best results, prepare add-ins immediately before using.

VIETNAMESE CHICKEN ASPARAGUS SOUP
Minh's Soup

MUSHROOM BARLEY SOUP

This is a very rich tasting, soul-satisfying soup - yet not high in calories or fat. If you can't find the frozen mushrooms, add fresh sliced mushrooms.

INGREDIENTS

Vegetables
2 onions, diced
2 leeks, washed well and diced
2 turnips, diced
4 carrots, diced
1 ounce dried mushrooms
1 package frozen mixed wild mushrooms
   (or 1 lb. fresh mushrooms, sliced or chopped)

Broth and Barley
½ cup white wine
1 tablespoon chicken *Better Than Bouillon*
4 turkey necks
1-2 cups barley (up to 2 cups for thicker soup)
1 teaspoon salt
8 cups water
4 tablespoons extra virgin olive oil

INSTRUCTIONS

1. Mix the *Better Than Bouillon* with 1 cup of water and the white wine in a medium pot. Add the dried mushrooms, and then bring the mixture to a boil. Turn off the heat, cover the pot and let it stand for ½ hour. After ½ hour, remove and slice the mushrooms – then return sliced mushrooms to the pot and set aside.
2. Brown the turkey necks in a large soup pot on a high heat and then add the rest of the water, the salt and the mushroom mixture from step 1. Bring the broth to a boil, and then turn the heat down to low and simmer.
3. While the soup pot is simmering, dice the onions and leeks.
4. Sauté the onions and leeks in olive oil in a separate pot until the onions become transparent. Add them, along with the barley, to the soup pot and continue simmering for a total of 2 hours.
5. After the two hours of simmering, add the diced turnips, carrots and mixed mushrooms. Bring the soup to a boil again and then reduce the heat to a simmer for a final 30 minutes.
6. Serve immediately or keep the soup in the refrigerator for up to 1 week.

For a vegetarian version, omit the turkey necks and substitute Vegetarian *Better Than Bouillon*.

YEMENITE CHICKEN SOUP

Yet another take on chicken soup, this recipe brings out the flavors of Yemenite cooking.

INGREDIENTS

Vegetables
4 carrots, chopped
6 cloves garlic, whole
2 onions, diced
2 turnips, chopped
2 stalks celery, chopped
3 zucchini or yellow squash, chopped

The Rest
4 chicken legs and 4 thighs, with skin and bones
1 turkey neck or wing
1 tablespoon chicken *Better Than Bouillon*
⅓ cup barley (optional)
2 tablespoons Yemenite soup spice*
1 teaspoon salt
1 tablespoon tomato paste
10 cups water

INSTRUCTIONS

1. Brown the chicken and turkey in a stock pot on high heat.
2. Cover meat with the water.
3. Bring the water to a boil and then skim off the excess chicken fat from the top of the broth.
4. Add the salt, chicken *Better Than Bouillon*, Yemenite soup spice, tomato paste, garlic, barley and onions.
5. Reduce heat and simmer for 2 hours.
6. After the soup has simmered for 2 hours, scoop out chicken and turkey pieces. Take the meat off the bone, remove the skin and discard both bones and skin. Shred and return meat to the pot.
7. Add the rest of the chopped vegetables (carrots, turnips, celery and squash), and bring the soup to a boil.
8. Reduce the heat and simmer for another 30 minutes.
9. Leave the soup to cool.
10. This soup will keep well in the refrigerator for up to 1 week.

*Available at Persian or Middle Eastern markets

Main Dishes

APRICOT BRANDY CHICKEN

This is a revamped version of my old recipe for Duck. I often make it with chicken, which is easier and more universally popular. It also works with Cornish game hens (one per person).

INGREDIENTS

Birds   1 small chicken (fryer)
            6 chicken thighs, bone-in and skin-on

Sauce   ¾ cup brandy (plain, apricot or peach)
            ¾ cup white wine
            1 large bottle of peaches in juice (24 oz.)
            Juice and zest of 1 orange
            1 teaspoon salt
            ¼ teaspoon pepper
            Extra virgin olive oil for sautéing onions
            25 golf ball sized onions, peeled, trimmed and left whole
            1 cup dried apricots, cut in half

INSTRUCTIONS

1. Preheat oven to 400°F.
2. Place chicken in a deep roasting pan and bake uncovered for 1 hour.
3. Sauté onions in olive oil until lightly browned (they will finish cooking in the oven)
4. Place all sauce ingredients, except for dried apricots, into a blender and puree until smooth.
5. Remove chicken from oven and reduce heat to 350°. Add onions to pan with chicken.
6. Pour sauce over chicken, top with apricot halves and return to the oven. Bake, covered, for an additional 2 hours. Remove from oven and serve.

On the way to the oven

Ready to serve

BONELESS SHORT RIBS OR BRISKET

Easy and delicious – a crowd pleaser! If there are any leftovers, shred the beef and serve over pasta as you would a ragù.

INGREDIENTS

6 lbs. boneless beef short ribs or brisket

Marinade:
2 tablespoons sweet smoked paprika
2 tablespoons ground ginger
2 tablespoons chili powder
3 garlic cloves, crushed
¼ cup extra virgin olive oil

A bottle of your favorite BBQ sauce

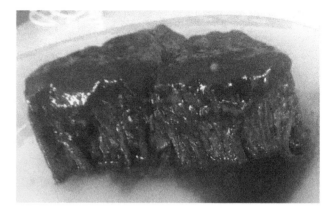

INSTRUCTIONS

1. Combine all marinade ingredients and rub into the meat. Place in heavy plastic bag and refrigerate for 12-24 hours.
2. Preheat oven to 300°F.
3. Bake marinated beef in a covered roasting pan for 3 hours.
4. Allow to cool, then cover and refrigerate for 2-24 hours.
5. If using brisket, slice against the grain when cold and place back in pan.
6. Cover meat with your favorite BBQ sauce.
7. Cover and bake at 350°F for 1 hour. It will be so tender you won't need a knife.

IRAQI SLOW-BAKED CHICKEN AND RICE – T'BEET

This recipe is adapted from my mother-in-law's version. She used white rice instead of the brown rice with lentils. She also stuffed the chicken with rice filling, and insisted on cooking it overnight instead of "only" 3 hours. I've never met anyone who didn't like this dish, and when we visited Safta Chaviva in Israel, T'beet was always the first dish my children asked her to make. This is a typical Iraqi Jewish dish served on the Sabbath, when cooking is prohibited. The casserole is prepared on Friday and cooked overnight with very low heat, resulting in tender chicken and deeply flavorful rice.

INGREDIENTS

1 5-pound chicken <u>or</u> 12 chicken thighs (bone-in)
2 cups brown rice
1 cup lentils, green or black
3 cups water
2 onions, chopped
¼ cup olive oil
2 teaspoons salt
2 teaspoons T'beet seasoning (also called
   Iraqi Meatball Seasoning, Pereg brand)
2 tablespoons tomato paste <u>or</u> 1 fresh tomato, diced
2 cups chicken or vegetable stock (boxed)
6 small potatoes
15 baby onions (optional)

INSTRUCTIONS

1. Cover the rice and lentils with water and soak overnight.
2. In the morning, drain and rinse the rice and lentils. Put the rice, lentils, 1 teaspoon of salt and 3 cups of water in a pot and bring the water to a boil.
3. Reduce heat and cover the pot. Cook the rice and lentils on a very low heat for 50 minutes.
4. Sauté chopped onions in the olive oil in a saucepan over medium heat until transparent.
5. Add the T'beet seasoning and 1 teaspoon salt to the onions and continue to sauté for another minute.
6. Add tomato paste and stock to onion mixture and continue to cook until it comes to a boil.
7. Set aside about a quarter of the tomato mixture.
8. Add the cooked rice to the remaining tomato mixture and put into the roasting pan.
9. Put the chicken on top of the mixture in a large roasting pan. Place the potatoes (and baby onions) around the chicken and then spoon the remaining tomato mixture over the chicken.
10. Cover the roasting pan and bake at 350° for 3 hours <u>OR</u> bake at 350° for ½ hour, then reduce the heat to 150° and allow it to cook overnight.
11. Serve hot.

PAD THAI

This is a fun dish that gets high marks with young and old alike. It has a lot more vegetables than the ones at Thai restaurants, but that's just fine with me!

INGREDIENTS

Vegetables and eggs	½ pound fresh sugar snap peas, diced 1 large or 2 small zucchini, diced ½ pound baby bok choy, chopped 2 eggs, beaten Toasted sesame oil
Noodles	1 pound dried flat rice noodles
Sauce	½ cup bottled Pad Thai sauce 2 tablespoons sweet chili sauce 2 tablespoons almond butter* 2 tablespoons toasted sesame oil ½ teaspoon Sriracha sauce or more, to taste
Garnishes for serving	Thai basil Fresh mint leaves Scallions, sliced Mung bean sprouts (optional) Sriracha sauce

INSTRUCTIONS

1. Sauté vegetables in sesame oil until just tender. Remove to a plate and reserve.
2. Add beaten eggs, scramble and chop with spatula. Remove to plate with vegetables.
3. Soak rice noodles in a bowl of hot water to "cook" by rehydrating.
4. Add a little more oil to the pan with cooked rice noodles and sauce. Return the vegetables and eggs to the wok, heat and stir. Serve hot.
5. Pass garnishes at the table for diners to choose and add.

(Peanut butter and chopped peanuts may be used if desired)

PAD THAI

POLLO A MATTONE
Chicken under a brick

This is probably my all time favorite dish. I tried making it many times before I was able to recreate the level of taste and texture I remember in Italy. I adapted this recipe from one that Nancy Silverton brought back from a trip she took to Italy and voila…this is it!!!

INGREDIENTS

Bird and marinade
- 12 bone in, skin on chicken thighs and/or chicken breast halves
- ½ cup Italian salad dressing (bottled or home made)
- 2 cloves garlic, crushed
- Zest of one lemon (organic)

Salsa Verde
- 1 Meyer lemon (organic), cut into ¼ inch wide slices and seeded
- 1 tablespoon extra virgin olive oil (for roasting lemon slices)
- 2 tablespoons pesto (without cheese)
- 1 teaspoon capers
- HRPF - hot red pepper flakes, to taste
- ½ cup extra virgin olive oil

INSTRUCTIONS

1. Assemble marinade and pour over chicken in a heavy plastic bag, distributing marinade well. Refrigerate overnight.
2. Preheat oven to 450°F and lay out lemon slices tossed with olive oil on a baking tray. Bake for 15-18 minutes, until charred on the bottom. Allow to cool enough to chop them in to ¼ inch dice, then add remaining salsa ingredients. Set aside.
3. Heat a large skillet and have a heavy weight ready (another skillet weighed down with a brick or other heavy weight).
4. Place marinated chicken in the hot skillet and cover with the second skillet and weight, pressing down on chicken.
5. Cook for 30-45 minutes over medium heat until browned, then turn chicken and repeat.
6. Serve topped with Salsa Verde. If made ahead, place in baking dish, cover with Salsa Verde and reheat in a 400°F oven.

POLLO A MATTONE
Chicken under a brick

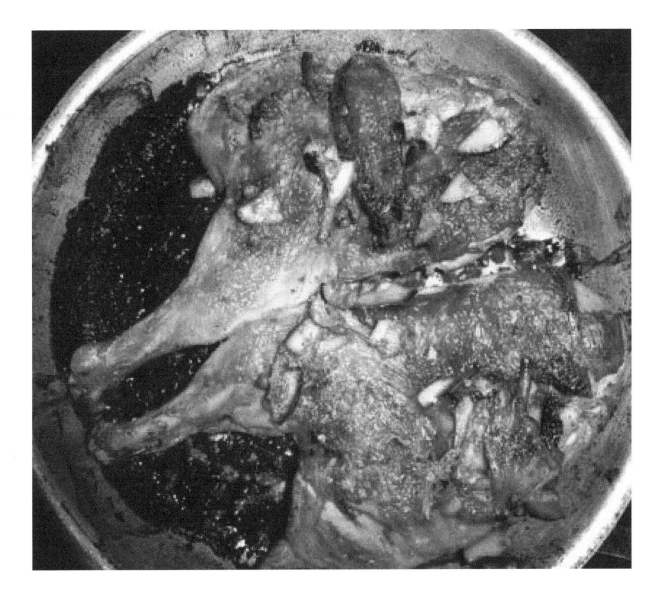

ROAST CHICKEN WITH PISTACHIO SALSA

The original recipe for this dish came from a chef from the French Laundry, a wonderful restaurant in Napa Valley, California. I have made the marinade bolder and simplified the salsa. It's beautiful and delicious and always gets rave reviews.

INGREDIENTS

Birds   2 whole chickens (3-4 pounds each)

Marinade   ¼ cup fresh squeezed lemon juice
Zest of one lemon (organic)
¼ cup extra virgin olive oil
3 cloves garlic, crushed
2 tablespoons dry salad dressing mix (Penzey's Italian or French Country)

Herbs   4 sprigs fresh rosemary, rinsed and dried

Salsa   ½ cup shelled pistachios, roasted and salted
½ cup chopped fresh chives
Zest of one lemon (organic)
½ cup extra virgin olive oil

INSTRUCTIONS

1. Make marinade in a small bowl.
2. Put each whole chicken in a plastic bag and pour half of marinade over each chicken, making sure marinade is distributed to coat chickens well. Seal bags and refrigerate for 4-24 hours. Massage chickens in sealed bags to aid distribution of marinade.
3. Preheat oven to 450°F.
4. Transfer chickens to roasting pan or to BBQ grill on wire stands.
5. Stuff each chicken with 2 sprigs of rosemary (in the neck end, on top when on the wire rack).
6. Roast at 450°F until well browned, 30-35 minutes.
7. Reduce heat to 350°F and continue roasting until thermometer reads 165°, about 30 minutes more.
8. Transfer to carving board and let rest.
9. Make pistachio salsa.
10. Carve chickens into serving portions.
11. Serve chicken with pistachio salsa on the side.

ROAST CHICKEN WITH PISTACHIO SALSA

ROAST CHICKEN WITH GREEN OLIVES AND APRICOTS

This recipe has become a real favorite with all the members of our extended family....even the extra picky ones! The combination of sweet, savory, sour and spicy really works.

INGREDIENTS

Birds   2 whole chickens (3-4 pounds each) or 12 chicken thighs (bone in)

Sauce   ¼ cup extra virgin olive oil
4 carrots, diced
2 medium onions, diced OR
   25 golf ball sized onions, whole
3 celery stalks, diced
1 teaspoon ground cumin
¼ teaspoon cayenne, or more to taste
1 cup dried apricots, diced
1½ cups pitted green Manzanilla olives
1 cup chicken stock
½ cup orange juice concentrate, thawed
Zest and juice of one navel orange
6 scallions, sliced
Salt and pepper, to taste

INSTRUCTIONS

1. Preheat oven to 425°F.
2. Place chicken in a baking dish and sprinkle with salt and pepper.
3. Bake uncovered in 425°F oven for 1 hour.
4. While the chicken is roasting, prepare the sauce.
5. Sauté the onions in olive oil until lightly browned, then add other vegetables and fruit.
6. Sauté mixture for 5 minutes, add spices, chicken stock and orange juice concentrate.
7. Remove chicken from oven and lower temperature to 350°F. Pour sauce over chicken, cover and bake for 1 hour more.
8. Sprinkle with scallions and serve.

SHRIMP RISOTTO WITH ASPARAGUS, ARUGULA AND CHÈVRE

This classic risotto from Sandy Smith is cooked on the stovetop in a large heavy pot such as Le Creuset. While time consuming, it is worth the effort for a special occasion!

INGREDIENTS

7 cups chicken stock, low salt _or_
   4 cups chicken stock and 3 cups water
1 pound shrimp, peeled and deveined
   (fresh or frozen, preferably wild caught)
2 cups asparagus spears, 1 inch pieces
¼ cup extra virgin olive oil
1½ cups chopped onion
2 carrots, peeled and diced small
6 cloves garlic, minced
1½ cups Arborio rice
1 cup dry white wine
¼ cup fresh squeezed lemon juice
5 ounces baby arugula leaves
1 ounce fresh basil, torn into small pieces
4 ounces chevre, fresh and mild
Hot red pepper flakes for the table

INSTRUCTIONS

1. Bring chicken stock to a simmer in a medium saucepan. Add shrimp. Turn off heat, cover and let stand until shrimp are just opaque, about 3-5 minutes depending on size of shrimp.
2. Using a slotted spoon, transfer shrimp to a bowl and cover to keep warm.
3. Add asparagus to chicken stock, bring back to a simmer, and cook until just tender. Transfer asparagus pieces to the bowl with the shrimp, cover and set aside.
4. Keep stock on the lowest heat your burner will produce, just to keep it hot.
5. Heat oil in a heavy Dutch oven (enameled cast iron is ideal) and add onions and carrots. Sauté until tender, about 5 minutes. Add minced garlic and cook 1 more minute.
6. Add rice and stir until edge of rice is translucent but center is still opaque, 3 or 4 minutes. A wooden spatula with a straight edge is ideal for scraping the bottom of the pot to avoid sticking. Add wine and continue to stir until wine is absorbed, 2 or 3 minutes.
7. Add about ¾ cup of hot chicken stock. Simmer until almost all stock is absorbed, stirring often. Continue to add stock, ¾ cup at a time, until rice is just tender and mixture is creamy, stirring often and allowing almost all the stock to be absorbed after each addition, about half an hour in total. Add lemon juice and stir to combine. The risotto should be slightly soupy.
8. Add arugula in about 4 big handfuls, stirring and allowing leaves to wilt after each addition. Stir in shrimp, asparagus and basil. Stir in chèvre.
9. Season to taste with salt and pepper. Spoon into shallow bowls and serve immediately, with hot red pepper flakes to pass at the table.
10. Leftovers can be diluted with additional chicken stock or water for a delicious soup. Reheat gently to keep the shrimp from becoming overcooked.

SOUTH CAROLINA BBQ CHICKEN

In the summer months, we BBQ frequently. This is a welcome change from the old standby tomato based sauce.

INGREDIENTS – MARINADE AND CHICKEN

2 cloves garlic, crushed
¼ cup whole grain mustard
1 teaspoon Dijon mustard
¼ cup molasses (or agave syrup)
1 tablespoon apple cider vinegar
1-2 teaspoons smoked salt
⅛ - ¼ teaspoon cayenne pepper, or more to taste
12 chicken thighs, skinned and boned

BASTING SAUCE

Cooking liquid from baking the chicken
1-2 tablespoons brown sugar
1 teaspoon sweet smoked paprika
1 teaspoon BBQ seasoning (dry spice mix such as Penzeys BBQ of America)
1 large shallot (or a small onion the size of an egg)
¼ teaspoon cayenne pepper, or more to taste
2 tablespoons apple cider vinegar

INSTRUCTIONS

1. Combine marinade and cover chicken thighs in a dish or zip lock bag.
2. Refrigerate for 12 to 24 hours.
3. Preheat oven to 350ºF.
4. Bake in a covered baking dish for 1 hour, then allow to cool to room temperature.
5. Remove chicken pieces to a plate and pour cooled cooking liquid into the blender.
6. Add remaining Basting Sauce ingredients and blend until smooth. Pour mixture into a saucepan and bring to a boil. Lower to a simmer and cook down to the consistency of ketchup, stirring frequently.
7. Cook chicken pieces on a hot grill, about 3 minutes per side. Baste with the sauce and grill about 2 minutes more on each side until caramelized.

SPAGHETTI CHICKEN

This simple dish was always a favorite of my children. While extremely easy to make and quick to prepare, this dish tastes like it was slaved over for hours.

INGREDIENTS

Meat
1 whole chicken or
   10 pieces of chicken, skinned

Vegetables and Mushrooms
1 onion, sliced
3 carrots, sliced
1 16 oz. package mushrooms, sliced
3 small zucchinis, sliced in half lengthwise
3 slender eggplants, sliced in half lengthwise
¼ cup extra virgin olive oil

Sauce
1 jar spaghetti sauce, 25-26 ounces
4 cloves garlic, crushed
2 teaspoon dried oregano
1 teaspoon dried basil
¼ teaspoon red pepper flakes or more, to taste

INSTRUCTIONS

1. Preheat the oven to 400°.
2. Sauté onions, carrots and mushrooms in olive oil for 5 minutes, then place in baking pan.
3. Lay the chicken on top of the vegetables.
4. Put the chicken and vegetables in the oven, uncovered, and bake at 400° for 30 minutes.
5. While the chicken and vegetables are in the oven, mix the *sauce* ingredients together in a saucepan over a low heat.
6. Remove the chicken and vegetables from the oven after 30 minutes and then pour the sauce over them.
7. Reduce oven temperature to 350°.
8. Cover the dish and return it to the oven.
9. Bake the dish at 350° while covered, for an additional 1 ½ hours.
10. While the dish is baking, brush the eggplant and zucchini slices with olive oil. Grill or broil them until nicely browned and just starting to char. Cut into bite sized slices.
11. Serve the chicken and sauce over al dente pasta. Top with eggplant and zucchini slices.

SPINACH CHICKEN AND RICE

Years ago we visited Pompeii, Italy. It was lunchtime; we were really hungry, and just happened to see a group of Italian grandmothers dressed all in black, sitting down to enjoy spinach pies. They offered us a taste, and I will never forget the amazing combination of flavors. I decided to try to make a chicken dish using these ingredients and here is the happy result. You can substitute Swiss chard for the spinach if preferred.

INGREDIENTS

Bird	1 whole chicken, *plus* 6 chicken thighs, skinned, bone in
Marinade	2 tablespoons pesto sauce (without cheese) HRPF - hot red pepper flakes – ¼ teaspoon or more, to taste ¼ cup extra virgin olive oil
Rice	2 cups brown rice, soaked overnight in cold water, rinsed and drained 1½ cups water 1 teaspoon salt 1 teaspoon vegetable *Better Than Bouillon*
Vegetables and Fruit	2 onions, diced ¼ cup extra virgin olive oil 3 bags (5 oz. each) organic baby spinach 1 large bunch fresh basil, washed and chopped 1 cup Kalamata olives, pitted

INSTRUCTIONS

1. Make up marinade and use it to coat chicken in a sturdy plastic bag. Marinate for 2-24 hours in the refrigerator.
2. Soak rice overnight in cold water.
3. Drain and rinse soaked rice, and place in 3 quart sauce pan with water, salt and bouillon. Bring to a boil, reduce heat to a simmer, cover and cook for 1 hour, or until tender.
4. Sauté onions in olive oil until starting to brown.
5. Preheat oven to 350°F.
6. Place cooked rice in large roasting pan, spreading it over the bottom. Add vegetables and olives, and mix with the rice.
7. Place marinated chicken over mixture, cover and bake for 2 hours.

VEAL STEW

This stew is a more economical version of Veal Osso Buco, and has tons of flavor. Long a family favorite, Mor's husband Joel always requests this when they come to visit.

INGREDIENTS

Vegetables and fresh herbs:
4 carrots, chopped
2 stalks celery, chopped
2 onions, chopped
4 cloves garlic, crushed
1 tomato, processed in the blender
2-4 sprigs fresh rosemary
1 lb. mushrooms, sliced

The Rest:
3 lbs veal stew meat*
2 veal marrow bones*
¼ cup regular or gluten free flour
¼ cup olive oil
1 teaspoon dried basil
1 cup white wine
¼ teaspoon hot pepper flakes
1 tablespoon chicken *Better Than Bouillon*
½ cup water
1 teaspoon salt

INSTRUCTIONS

1. Preheat oven to 375°, and arrange oven racks low enough for casserole with lid.
2. Combine flour, basil and salt in a plate. Lightly coat meat and bones with the flour mixture.
3. Heat the oil in an ovenproof casserole or Dutch oven.
4. Sear the meat over a medium high flame until browned on all sides.
5. Remove meat from casserole to plate.
6. In the casserole, sauté the onions until transparent, then add carrots, rosemary sprigs, garlic and celery. Cook for 5 minutes.
7. Add the wine and continue cooking until to loosen any remaining pieces on the bottom.
8. Add the seared meat and pureed tomato, *Better Than Bouillon* and chili flakes. If the mixture looks dry, add approximately 1 cup of water, as needed.
9. Place the casserole in a preheated 375° oven and bake, covered, for 1½ hours.
10. Add the chopped mushrooms in the last 30 minutes of cooking.
11. Serve over rice or pasta, removing remaining rosemary twigs.

*Humanely raised veal is available online and in some meat departments. Beef stew meat or turkey thigh meat (boneless and skinless) may be substituted for the veal.

STUFFED ZUCCHINI TUNISIAN STYLE

This recipe is from my Tunisian sister in law, Mazal, who uses lots of Harissa to make it very spicy. I toned it down for my family's taste and it is a great favorite. It is easier to make than its cousin, stuffed cabbage, and looks beautiful when being served.

INGREDIENTS

10 zucchinis – small or medium (the light green ones are my favorite, but any color or a combination will work well)

Filling
1 lb. ground turkey or ground beef (or mixed)
1 bunch fresh flat leaf parsley, minced
¼ cup fresh dill, minced
1 medium onion, minced
1 cup uncooked brown rice, soaked overnight
1 tablespoon tomato paste
1 teaspoon salt
1 teaspoon cinnamon
2 teaspoons ground cumin
½ to 1 teaspoon Moroccan harissa
½ teaspoon curry powder (optional)

Sauce
¼ cup extra virgin olive oil
1 medium onion, chopped
2 cloves garlic, minced
1 teaspoon harissa
4 tablespoons tomato paste
1 teaspoon cinnamon
2 teaspoons ground cumin
¼ cup fresh squeezed lemon juice
2 to 4 tablespoons sugar
1 tablespoon chicken *Better Than Bouillon*
1 teaspoon salt
¼ cup Goji berries or raisins
5 cups water

INSTRUCTIONS

Filling
1. Soak rice in cold water overnight. Drain in the morning.
2. Cover the soaked rice with fresh water to about ½ inch above the rice. Add ½ teaspoon salt and bring to a boil.
3. Lower the heat and simmer until cooked, about 30 minutes. Allow cooked rice to cool.
4. Chop the onion, parsley and dill in a food processor until it smoothes out.
5. Add remaining filling ingredients and mix thoroughly. Set aside.

Zucchini and Sauce
1. Trim ends of zucchini and cut in half lengthwise. With a teaspoon, scoop out the soft center section, leaving about ¼ inch next to the skin. Set hollowed out zucchini aside. Keep the scooped out flesh.
2. Sauté onions and scooped out flesh with olive oil until onions are transparent. Add spices, stir well, and then add remaining ingredients. Simmer the sauce for about ½ hour.

Assembly and Baking
1. In a 9 x 13" baking dish, arrange zucchini halves and add filling. Spoon sauce over all and cover with aluminum foil. Bake at 350° for 1½ hours.
2. Leftovers keep in the refrigerator for a week. This does not freeze well – it gets watery.

STUFFED ZUCCHINI TUNISIAN STYLE

VIETNAMESE CHICKEN KEBABS

I am always happy to find new ways to make Kebab. This was inspired by an Israeli newspaper article about variations. All the flavor of Vietnamese egg rolls without the frying!

INGREDIENTS

1 pound ground chicken (or turkey)
½ bunch fresh mint, leaves only, washed
1 bunch green onions, trimmed
½ bunch Thai basil, leaves only, washed
1 clove garlic, crushed
1 tablespoon toasted sesame oil
1 tablespoon fresh ginger juice
   (fresh ginger, grated or put through a
   garlic press)
½ teaspoon salt
1 teaspoon Sriracha sauce, or more to taste
Fresh cilantro leaves as a garnish

INSTRUCTIONS

1. In a food processor, chop mint leaves, green onions and basil leaves until finely minced but not pureed.
2. Scoop herb mixture into a mixing bowl and add meat and remaining ingredients. Mix together with clean hands or a wooden spoon. Form into elongated patties about the size of a medium sized egg and about ¾ inch thick.
3. Grill on medium-high heat, 2 minutes on each side.
4. Serve in lettuce leaves with Vietnamese Cabbage Salad (p. 31). Sprinkle with cilantro leaves if desired.

Side Dishes

ARTICHOKE RICE

This recipe is especially wonderful in the Spring, when fresh basil is appearing in farmer's markets again. But happily, basil is now available year round!

INGREDIENTS

2 cups brown rice, soaked overnight in cold water
2 cups water
1 tablespoon pesto (preferably without cheese)
1 teaspoon *Better than Bouillon*
1 cup fresh Italian basil, chopped
1 bunch fresh flat-leaf parsley, chopped
3 large chard leaves, chopped
1 teaspoon salt
¼ - 1 teaspoon harissa, to taste (optional)
2 onions, diced
¼ cup extra virgin olive oil
1 package Trader Joe's frozen artichoke hearts

INSTRUCTIONS

1. Sauté onion in olive oil until golden.
2. Add remaining ingredients and bring to a boil.
3. Cover and cook over a very low flame for 1 hour or until rice is cooked.
4. Serve immediately or transfer to a baking dish to be reheated for 30 minutes at 350°F.

BUTTERNUT SQUASH KUGEL

This a wonderful dish to serve in the fall, when butternut squash is in season. It is good for Thanksgiving because it is flavorful yet lighter than so many traditional Thanksgiving casseroles.

INGREDIENTS

1 large butternut squash, peeled and shredded
¼ teaspoon salt
5 eggs
½ cup extra virgin olive oil
¼ cup gluten free or regular flour
1 teaspoon cinnamon
2 tablespoons maple syrup or more, to taste
1 cup raisins

INSTRUCTIONS

1. Prepare a baking dish with cooking oil spray.
2. Preheat oven to 325°F.
3. In a large mixing bowl, lightly beat eggs with salt. Mix in oil and flour.
4. Add remaining ingredients and combine.
5. Scoop into prepared baking dish and bake for 1 hour.

BUTTERNUT SQUASH RICE

This dish is easy to make and the natural sweetness makes it a no-fail way to get kids to eat their vegetables.

INGREDIENTS

Squash Rice Mixture
1 medium butternut squash, peeled and put through the dicer disc in a food processor
2 cups brown rice, soaked overnight in cold water, rinsed and drained
2 cups water
1 teaspoon salt
1 teaspoon chicken soup broth (*Better Than Bouillon* brand)
1 teaspoon agave syrup or brown sugar

Add-ins
2 onions, chopped fine
½ cup extra virgin olive oil
¾ cup raisins (optional)

Garnish
½ cup toasted almonds (optional)

INSTRUCTIONS

1. Combine the *Squash Rice Mixture* ingredients in a large pot and bring to a boil. Reduce heat and simmer gently for one hour, covered.
2. Sauté onions in olive oil until brown.
3. Add raisins and fold into cooked *Squash Rice Mixture*.
4. Top with almonds and serve.

GRILLED ARTICHOKES

When fresh artichokes are in season…!

INGREDIENTS

12 small fresh artichokes
1 lemon, quartered
Extra virgin olive oil for brushing artichokes
Salt to taste

INSTRUCTIONS
1. Snap off the hard outer leaves, leaving the base intact.
2. When you get to the tender light green leaves, cut off the top of the choke with the thorn.
3. Cut in half and remove the inner hairs (if there are any). Leave the stems on.
4. Place trimmed artichokes in a bowl of water with the lemon wedges to prevent discoloration.
5. Place artichokes in salted boiling water for 5 minutes. Drain well and place on paper towels to dry.
6. Brush with olive oil and sprinkle with salt.
7. Grill (or broil) until browned and serve.

In the lemon water bath

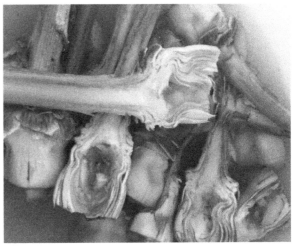

Boiled before grilling

HEALTHY FRIED RICE

This version of fried rice is delicious with much less oil than the restaurant classic.

INGREDIENTS

2 cups brown rice, soaked overnight
  in cold water
1 teaspoon salt
4 cups water
4 medium carrots, diced
1 cup sliced sugar snap peas
1 bunch green onions, sliced
2 tablespoons avocado oil
2 tablespoons tamari sauce
2 tablespoons toasted sesame oil

INSTRUCTIONS

1. Drain soaked rice. Place in saucepan with water and salt , bring to a boil, cover and reduce heat to low. Cook for 1 hour, until tender. Place cooked rice in a strainer and then return to the pot for about 10 minutes.
2. Flash fry the carrots in avocado oil for 2 minutes. Remove to a bowl.
3. Flash fry the sugar snap peas in the same manner.
4. Flash fry the green onions for 10 seconds and remove to bowl.
5. Fold vegetables into cooked rice along with tamari sauce and sesame oil.
6. Serve hot.

IRAQI RICE AND FAVA BEANS

This is a typical Jewish Iraqi rice dish. It is usually served during Passover, when fava beans are at their peak. Today you can buy frozen fava beans to enjoy all year. For those people with sensitivity to tomatoes, be assured it is delicious and super nutritious to use macerated Swiss chard instead.

INGREDIENTS

1½ cups fresh or frozen fava beans,
   removed from pods
2 cups brown rice, soaked overnight in
   cold water
3 cups water
1 teaspoon salt
1 teaspoon *Better than Bouillon*
1 tablespoon tomato paste (or 4 large
   leaves Swiss chard, chopped fine)
¼ - 1 teaspoon harissa, to taste
1 large onion, diced
¼ cup olive oil

INSTRUCTIONS

1. Sauté onion in olive oil until browned. Add fava beans and sauté for 1 more minute.
2. Add remaining ingredients and bring to a boil.
3. Cover and cook over a low flame for 1 hour or until rice is cooked.
4. Serve immediately or put in a baking dish to be reheated for 30 minutes at 350°F.

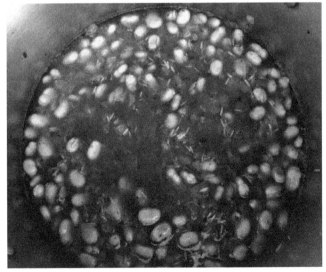

In step 2, the fava beans are still green

MEJEDERA
Rice and Lentils with Crispy Onions

In this version of a classic rice and lentil dish, the onions are broiled, not fried.

INGREDIENTS

1 cup lentils
2 cups brown basmati rice
1 teaspoon salt
3 cups water
½ teaspoon harissa, or more to taste
1 teaspoon Vegetable *Better than Bouillon*
½ cup extra virgin olive oil, divided
4 onions, 2 chopped and 2 sliced into thin rings
3 tablespoons flour (regular or gluten free)
2 teaspoons ground cumin
1 bunch fresh parsley, washed and dried
4-6 chard leaves, washed and dried

INSTRUCTIONS

1. Soak lentils and rice in cold water overnight. Drain and rinse well.
2. Finely chop parsley and chard in a food processor.
3. Place rice, lentils, water, salt, harissa, parsley and chard in a large pot. Bring to a boil, then turn down to a simmer and cook, covered, for 1 hour or until rice is tender.
4. Sauté chopped onions in ¼ cup olive oil until golden. Add cumin and stir to combine. Add onion mixture to cooked rice and mix well.
5. Gently toss raw onion rings with ¼ cup olive oil to coat. Dredge in flour and spread on cookie sheet. Broil until crispy. Spread crispy onion rings on top of rice in serving dish.

MUSHROOM RICE

I love risotto but not how labor intensive it is to make. This rice dish mimics a risotto with a quarter of the effort. It's perfect to make for guests because you make it ahead and reheat.

INGREDIENTS

2 cups brown rice (soaked overnight in cold water, rinsed and drained)
1½ cups water
¼ cup dried mushrooms, soaked in ½ cup hot water (bring to a boil, remove from heat, cover and allow to cool)
1 onion, diced and fried in ¼ cup extra virgin olive oil
8 ounces white or Crimini mushrooms, sliced
12 ounce package frozen mushroom medley (Trader Joe's)
1 teaspoon vegetable bouillon (*Better Than Bouillon* brand)
1 teaspoon salt

INSTRUCTIONS

1. Sauté onion until lightly browned.
2. Add fresh mushrooms and sauté 3-4 minutes, until softened.
3. Add frozen mushrooms and sauté 3-4 minutes (no need to thaw).
4. Add rice and liquids, salt and bouillon, then bring to a boil.
5. Cover rice mixture, lower heat to a simmer and cook for 30-60 minutes until rice is tender.
6. Remove to a Pyrex baking dish and allow to cool. Before serving, reheat in a 350°F oven for 20-30 minutes, uncovered. This second step is necessary to achieve the optimal consistency.

ROASTED SMALL ONIONS

I first had these onions when my company sponsored a trip to Great Britain and hosted a dinner for us at Hampton Court (the castle Henry VIII built for Anne Boleyn before he beheaded her). They were served as a side dish, with the meat. After a little experimentation, I was able to recreate their amazing taste!

INGREDIENTS

20 small (golf ball size) onions
¼ cup olive oil
2 tablespoons balsamic vinegar

INSTRUCTIONS

1. Preheat oven to 400°F.
2. Peal and trim ends from onions.
3. Pour olive oil into Pyrex dish and then roll onions around in it to coat.
4. Bake at 400°F until browned.
5. Drizzle with vinegar and turn off oven. Leave in oven until ready to serve.

SZECHUAN GREEN BEANS

This healthier version of a restaurant classic has become a family favorite at our house.

INGREDIENTS

½ pound green beans, trimmed
¼ cup water
1 tablespoon minced ginger
   (or Trader Joe's Ginger Paste)
2 cloves garlic, minced
2 tablespoons toasted sesame oil
2 tablespoons soy sauce or Tamari
1 tablespoon rice vinegar
½ teaspoon white sugar or Agave syrup
¼ teaspoon red pepper flakes (or more, to taste)

INSTRUCTIONS

1. Combine green beans and water in a skillet over medium high heat. Cover and cook, stirring occasionally, until beans are tender crisp, 4 to 5 minutes.
2. Drain beans and return to the pan.
3. Add ginger, garlic and sesame oil; cook, stirring frequently, until garlic is lightly browned, 1 to 2 minutes.
4. In a small bowl, whisk together soy sauce, vinegar, sugar and red pepper flakes. Pour over beans and cook until sauce thickens enough to coat beans, 3 to 5 minutes.

VEGETARIAN "FAT RICE"

A restaurant in Chicago serves a wildly popular – and very decadent - dish called "Fat Rice". This is a healthier, vegetarian version that retains all the levels of flavor. My vegetarian friends have given it their seal of approval!

INGREDIENTS & INSTRUCTIONS for rice:

2½ cups brown basmati rice, soaked overnight in cold water and then drained
1 bunch Swiss chard, minced in the food processor
2 tablespoons tomato paste or Moroccan Matbucha (see recipe on p. ___)
1 teaspoon hot sauce (I used sweet chili hot sauce)
1 teaspoon kosher or coarse salt
1 teaspoon vegetarian broth (*Better Than Bouillon* brand paste)
1 diced onion (yellow, white or brown)
¼ cup extra virgin olive oil
3 cups water

Sauté onion in oil until it begins to brown. Add the rest of the ingredients and bring to a rolling boil. Cover, reduce heat to lowest setting and cook for 1 hour.

INGREDIENTS & INSTRUCTIONS for vegetables, nuts and fruit to be mixed in:

While rice is cooking, prepare the following:
1 diced onion (yellow, white or brown)
¼ cup extra virgin olive oil
1 charred red bell pepper, diced after cooking (char skin of whole pepper under broiler or on the grill, remove to a paper bag for about 10 minutes, peel charred skin, remove seeds and core, then dice)
1 teaspoon smoked paprika
1 cup sliced almonds, lightly toasted
1 cup raisins
1-2 cups pitted olives (green or your favorite)
15 oz. can black beans, drained
3 scallions, sliced
1 cup green peas, cooked until just tender

Sauté diced onion in olive oil until well browned, then add the remaining ingredients. When mixture is heated through, add to cooked rice and toss well. Top with scallions and peas just before serving. Keep warm on low heat until ready to serve or if doing ahead, place in a baking dish and reheat covered at 350°F for 30 to 45 minutes.

VEGETARIAN "FAT RICE"

VEGETABLES WITH TAHINI SAUCE

This is a popular dish served in restaurants in Israel today. It is served as a main dish for vegetarians, using one large eggplant per serving. An Israeli friend, Valentina, taught me how to make it after I raved about it at her house.

INGREDIENTS

Vegetables   10 small zucchini (5 inches or less)
10 small, slender eggplants (5 inches or less)
Extra virgin olive oil for brushing on vegetables

Tahini Sauce   ½ cup sesame seed paste
½ teaspoon salt
1 clove garlic, crushed
Juice of 1 lemon
¼-½ cup water

INSTRUCTIONS

1. Wash and dry zucchini and eggplants. Trim ends.
2. Cut zucchini and eggplants in half lengthwise and arrange in a shallow roasting pan, cut side up. Carefully slash the top of each half with three X marks, about ⅛" deep.
3. Brush the cut side with olive oil and broil on high until nicely browned.
4. Prepare Tahini Sauce in a food processor, pureeing all ingredients until smooth. Add more water if needed to achieve the consistency of ketchup.
5. Just before serving, spoon Tahini Sauce over top of veggies and bake at 400ºF for 5-10 minutes.
6. Serve hot.

Desserts
&
Other Sweets

ALMOND COOKIES
Gluten free

These are great for Passover, but they're so good you'll want to make them all year round.

INGREDIENTS

Almond mixture	2 8-ounce packages thin sliced almonds
	3 egg whites
	¾ cup granulated sugar
	1 teaspoon vanilla extract
	Grated rind of 1 organic orange
Optional additions (choose one)	1 cup chocolate chips (mini if available)
	1 cup raisins
	1 cup dried cranberries

INSTRUCTIONS

1. Preheat the oven to 350°.
2. Mix (do not beat) the egg whites and sugar in a bowl with a fork.
3. Add the rest of the ingredients, including any optional add-ins, and mix well.
4. Line a cookie sheet with silpat or parchment and spoon out <u>teaspoons</u> full of the mixture onto the cookie sheet.
5. Place the cookie sheet in the oven and bake for 10–15 minutes at 350°, until the cookies are golden brown.
6. Remove the cookie sheet and let the cookies cool completely.
7. Store in airtight containers.
8. Cookies will last up to 1 month.

APPLE BERRY PIE WITH ALMOND TOPPING
Gluten-free

This is an adaptation of an apple recipe given to Sandy Smith by her Swedish friend Ingrid Munck. It just happens to be gluten free and low in sugar. It is beautiful and delicious. It also goes well with a scoop of vanilla ice cream!

INGREDIENTS
7-8 large tart apples (e.g. Pink Lady)
1 cup dark sweet cherries, pitted and
    quartered (frozen cherries are fine)
1 cup blueberries (fresh or frozen)
1 stick of salted butter, room temperature:
        7 tablespoons for batter
        1 tablespoon to generously coat a
        large pie plate
½ cup sugar
1¼ cups almond meal
1 large organic lemon, zest and juice
1 scant tablespoon almond extract
2 whole eggs, plus 1 egg white

INSTRUCTIONS
1. Peel and slice the apples about ¼" thick. Quarter the cherries.
2. Steam the fruit until the apples are just softened, then scoop fruit out with a slotted spoon and cool in a bowl (warm is OK, but not still hot). <u>Do not discard the water used for steaming!</u>
3. Boil the steaming water (now purple from the cherries and blueberries) until reduced and thickened into syrup. There will be about ½ cup or so. Watch that it doesn't scorch.
4. Butter a large pie plate and add cooled fruit. Pour syrup over fruit and set aside.
5. Preheat oven to 375°F, with rack in the center.
6. In a bowl, cream butter and sugar together. Mix in almond meal.
7. Add the almond extract, lemon zest and juice. Add egg yolks one at a time. If it seems too dry, add more lemon juice.
8. Whip the three egg whites until stiff but not dry and gently fold them into the batter.
9. Pour the batter over the fruit. Smooth to an even thickness with a rubber spatula.
10. Bake in the middle of the oven for 30-35 minutes, or until nicely golden. Watch that it doesn't get too brown – the topping can become dry.
11. Serve as is, or with vanilla ice cream. Room temperature is ideal.

NOTE: The combination of fruit can be varied according to preference or availability. It would also be good with raspberries, blackberries, etc., added to the apples.

ALSATIAN APPLE ALMOND CAKE
Gluten free, Dairy free

This lovely apple cake is mostly fruit, held together with a delicate eggy batter. The original version used regular flour, but it works beautifully with the almond flour, which makes it both gluten-free and higher in protein. It is excellent for breakfast with coffee or tea, as well as for dessert. Choose apples that won't turn to mush when cooked.

INGREDIENTS

Cake
- 4 lbs. baking apples (e.g. Pink Lady)
- 3 jumbo or 4 large eggs
- ⅓ cup mild flavored honey (e.g. Orange Blossom)
- ¼ cup grapeseed or extra virgin olive oil
- 1 teaspoon vanilla extract
- 2 tablespoons rum or compatible favorite liquor
- 1 cup flour: ½ cup almond flour and ½ cup gluten-free or regular flour, or all almond flour, as preferred
- 1 teaspoon cinnamon (optional)
- 1 tablespoon baking powder
- 1 teaspoon baking soda
- Pinch of salt
- 1 tablespoon butter for cake pan (or cooking oil spray)

Topping
- 1 egg
- 2 tablespoons butter, melted and slightly cooled (or coconut oil)
- 3 tablespoons brown sugar
- 1 teaspoon cinnamon (optional)

ALSATION APPLE ALMOND CAKE

INSTRUCTIONS FOR ONE LARGE CAKE

1. Preheat oven to 425°F. Generously butter a large cake pan (12 inch cake pan or 10 inch spring form pan).
2. Peel, core and cut the apples into even slices, about ¼ inch thick. Place in a large bowl.
3. In a smaller bowl, whisk together eggs, honey, oil, vanilla and rum.
4. Whisk together flour, cinnamon, baking powder, baking soda and salt. Stir into egg mixture until smooth.
5. Pour batter over the apples and stir gently to coat. Turn into buttered cake pan.
6. Bake for 30 minutes.
7. While the cake is baking, mix the topping ingredients together. Mix the egg, sugar and cinnamon together first, and then dribble in the slightly cooled melted butter gradually so as not to cook the egg. When the cake has baked for 30 minutes, remove from the oven and pour on the topping as evenly as possible. Return to the oven for about 10 minutes more, until topping is caramelized.
8. Cool in the pan on a wire rack
9. Serve warm or cool. Refrigerate for storage. It reheats well.

INSTRUCTIONS FOR INDIVIDUAL SIZE SERVINGS

Follow the instructions above, with the following changes:

- Preheat oven to 350°F instead of 425°.
- Line regular sized muffin tins with paper liners and spray the liners with cooking oil spray. Makes 24 muffin-sized cakes.
- Cut apple slices in half for shorter pieces that will fit into muffin cups.

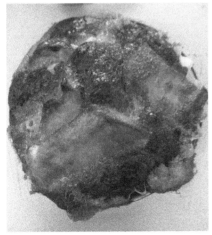
Individual portion

Individual portion with nectarines

APPLE CAKE
Helen Rowe

My mother, Helen Rowe, made this cake for special occasions and it was always popular. She didn't care how much butter she used, as long as it tasted good... and it really does taste good.

INGREDIENTS

Cake   6 cups tart apples, shredded (peels left on)
¼ pound butter (1 stick) plus 1 tablespoon for preparing cake pan
½ cup sour cream (may use non-dairy sour cream or yogurt)
Grated zest and juice of 1 lemon
1 cup sugar
¼ cup flour (regular or gluten free)
½ cup thinly sliced almonds
8 egg yolks
1 teaspoon vanilla extract
8 egg whites

Topping   ½ cup sugar
4 teaspoons cinnamon
1 cup thinly sliced almonds

INSTRUCTIONS

1. Prepare large (12 inch) spring form pan with softened butter.
2. Melt stick of butter in a 3 quart saucepan, and then mix in shredded apples.
3. Combine remaining cake ingredients (except for eggs) and cook in saucepan until thickened. Allow to cool to lukewarm. Whisk egg yolks in a bowl and then whisk into cooled batter.
4. Preheat oven to 350°F.
5. Beat egg whites until they form soft peaks.
6. Fold egg whites into batter and pour into buttered spring form pan.
7. Assemble topping ingredients and spread over batter.
8. Bake for 1 hour and test with a toothpick. Cool in pan on wire rack and then refrigerate.
9. Serve cold or room temperature, storing leftovers in refrigerator.

APRICOT PECAN LOAF
Gluten free

This a wonderful treat to make when apricots come into season. If you are desperate for some in the dead of winter, you can make it with frozen apricots as well.

INGREDIENTS

Dry Ingredients	2 cups gluten free flour
	1 heaping teaspoon baking powder
	1 heaping teaspoon baking soda
	Pinch of salt
Fruit and Nuts	1 cup fresh apricot puree (Trader Joe's or Whole Foods - in jars)
	6 fresh apricots, washed, pitted and diced
	1 cup dried apricots, diced
	1 cup chopped pecans
Wet ingredients and pecans	½ cup coconut oil
	1 cup coconut sugar
	2 teaspoons vanilla extract
	2 eggs or egg substitute
	2 tablespoons non-dairy yogurt (regular plain yogurt may be used if desired)
	½ cup agave syrup

INSTRUCTIONS

1. Preheat oven to 325°F.
2. Prepare 4 small loaf pans with cooking oil spray.
3. Whisk *dry ingredients* together in a medium bowl and set aside.
4. Prepare apricots as described.
5. In a large mixing bowl, beat coconut oil and sugar together, then add remaining wet ingredients and mix until well blended.
6. Add dry ingredients and incorporate until batter is smooth.
7. Add apricots and pecans.
8. Divide batter into loaf pans. Bake for about 60 minutes or until a toothpick comes out clean.
9. Remove from pans and cool loaves on a wire rack.

AVOCADO LIME PIE
Vegan and Gluten-free

After many attempts to create a Lime Pie for those of us who can't have dairy, success at last! It is wonderful, if I do say so myself.

INGREDIENTS

Crust &
Topping
2 cups pecans – toasted until lightly browned and fragrant
2 tablespoons agave syrup or honey
2 teaspoons vanilla extract

Filling
1 cup fresh squeezed lime juice from about 2 pounds of limes
Zest of one medium lime
¾ cup agave syrup (rice syrup or sugar would also work)
½ cup coconut milk (shake can well before adding)
2 ½ cups ripe green avocados (discard any brown spots)
2 teaspoons vanilla extract
¼ teaspoon salt
3 tablespoons lecithin granules
¾ cup coconut oil

INSTRUCTIONS

1. Place crust ingredients in a food processor and chop into even sized crumbs.
2. Press about ¾ of the crumbs into the bottom of a 9" spring form pan or 10 small ramekins. Set aside remaining crumbs.
3. Place filling ingredients in blender and blend until smooth.
4. Pour filling over the crust(s) and top with remaining crust mixture, crumbled (not pressed).
5. Refrigerate overnight. Serve cold!

BABA
Iraqi Date Cookies

My children have fond memories of their grandfather, Saba Itzhak, visiting from Israel, rising early in the morning and assembling all his "tools". He would sit in the kitchen for hours making hundreds of Baba to store in our freezer. Baba is the perfect semi-sweet snack for a quick tea or coffee break - any time, day or night.

INGREDIENTS

Filling	Dough
2 packages (13 ounces each) pressed dates	3½ cups whole wheat pastry flour
1-2 teaspoons cinnamon	4 cups unbleached white flour
1-2 teaspoons vanilla extract	½ cup extra virgin olive oil
2-3 tablespoons extra virgin olive oil	1 teaspoon salt
	1 package dry yeast
	4 tablespoons sugar
	Warm water as needed
	1 cup sesame seeds (for topping)

INSTRUCTIONS

Filling
1. Place all the filling ingredients into a saucepan and heat on a low flame. Stir continually until all the ingredients are well blended.
2. Set aside and let the filling cool.

Dough
1. Dissolve the yeast and 1 teaspoon of sugar in a cup of warm water and let it rise.
2. Add the yeast mixture to the rest of the dry ingredients (not the sesame seeds) and knead the dough until it becomes smooth.
3. Place the dough in a bowl and cover it with a dish towel. Let rise for 1 hour.

Assembly and Baking
1. Preheat the oven to 355°.
2. Pinch off pieces of the date mixture and roll them into marble sized balls.
3. Break off pieces of the dough, about an inch in diameter.
4. Flatten the dough in the palm of your hand and place a date ball in the center.
5. Close the dough, and completely encompass the date ball with the dough.
6. Lay the sesame seeds out on a plate.
7. Dip the ball in the plate of sesame seeds and then roll out each ball into a thin disk.
8. Dimple the disk with the end of a wooden spoon or a rolling pin.
9. Place the disks on a baking sheet, seed side up.
10. Bake the Baba at 355°, until they are slightly golden, about 10 – 11 minutes.
11. Remove the cookies from the oven and cool them completely.
12. They can then be placed in freezer bags and frozen until ready to serve.
13. To reheat, simply put the desired number of frozen cookies in the toaster oven and toast on a light setting.

(turn page for a step by step guide)

BABA
Iraqi Date Cookies – step by step guide

Saba Itzhak making Baba

Baba dough, ready to use

Sesame seeds and date balls

Pinch off enough dough to cover date ball

Wrap dough around date ball

Flatten ball and dip one side in sesame seeds

86

BABA
Iraqi Date Cookies – step by step guide

Roll thin with seed side down

Make dimples with end of rolling pin

Place seed side up on cookie sheet

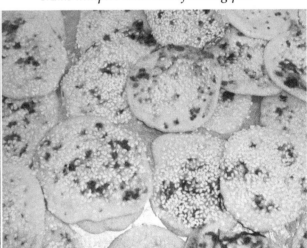

Par-baked cookies

Par-baked Baba, cooled and packed for freezer

Baba toasted and ready to eat

BABKA

Braided yeast cake with Chocolate Nut or Cinnamon Pecan Filling

The inspiration for this Babka (yeast cake) recipe came from Ottolenghi's book Jerusalem. I have tweaked it a bit, but I must say his method of making it, although involved, works well, and the result is both beautiful and delicious. Be sure not to leave off the syrup at the end. I tried that once and the result was disappointing. For nondairy cake you may use coconut oil, but it really is much better with butter! This recipe makes two large loaves; if you want to make one of each flavor, cut the filling ingredients by half. The cakes will keep for up to two days at room temperature, wrapped in foil, and up to a couple of weeks when frozen.

INGREDIENTS

Dough	4¼ cups all purpose flour (plus more for dusting)
	½ cup sugar
	1 package fast-rising active dry yeast
	Grated zest of 1 small lemon or orange (organic)
	3 extra-large eggs
	½ cup water
	¼ teaspoon salt, rounded
	⅔ cup unsalted butter, room temperature, cut into ½ inch cubes
	Sunflower or canola oil for preparing rising bowl and loaf pans
Chocolate filling	½ cup (scant) confectioners' sugar
	⅓ cup cocoa powder
	4½ ounces dark chocolate, melted
	8 tablespoons (1 stick) unsalted butter, melted
	1 teaspoon vanilla extract
	1 cup pecans (or walnuts), coarsely chopped
	2 tablespoons sugar
Cinnamon filling	6 tablespoons unsalted butter, melted
	¾ cup brown sugar
	1½ tablespoons ground cinnamon
	Zest of 1 lemon, organic
	2 cups pecans, chopped
Finishing Syrup	⅔ cup water
	1¼ cups sugar

BABKA

INSTRUCTIONS

1. **Dough:** Place the flour, sugar, yeast and lemon zest in a stand mixer. Mix with a dough hook on low speed for one minute. Add eggs and water and mix on low speed for a few seconds, then increase speed to medium and mix for 3 minutes, until the dough comes together. Add salt, and then add the butter a few cubes at a time until it is mixed in. Continue mixing for about 10 minutes on medium speed, or until the dough is completely smooth, elastic and shiny. During mixing, scrape down the sides of the bowl a few times and throw a small amount of flour onto the sides so that dough is not left in the bowl.

2. Oil a large bowl. Scoop dough out of mixer bowl and place in oiled bowl - then flip it over so that entire surface is oiled. Cover with plastic wrap and refrigerate overnight (or half a day at the very least).

3. Oil two 9x4" loaf pans and line the bottoms with waxed paper. Divide the dough in half. While working the first half, keep the other half covered and back in the refrigerator.

4. **Chocolate Filling:** Mix together the confectioners' sugar, cocoa powder, chocolate and butter. **Cinnamon Filling:** Mix the butter, sugar and cinnamon together. Each filling will be in the form of spreadable paste.

5. Roll out the dough on a lightly floured surface, making a rectangle measuring 15" by 11". Trim the sides to make them even. Position the dough so that a long side is closest to you. Spread half the chocolate or cinnamon mixture over the rectangle, leaving a ¾" border all around. For the **Chocolate**, sprinkle half the pecans on top of the paste, then sprinkle with half the sugar. For the **Cinnamon**, sprinkle the paste with half the lemon zest and pecans.

6. Brush the long end farthest away from you with a little water. Use both hands to roll up the rectangle like a roulade, starting from the long side closest to you and rolling it toward the far end. Press to seal the dampened end onto the roll and then use both hands to even out the roll. Rest the roll on its seam.

7. With the serrated knife, gently cut the roll in half, lengthwise, starting at the top and finishing at the seam. You will have two long halves, exposing the layers along the length of the pieces. With the cut sides facing up, gently press together one end of each half, then lift the right half over the left half. Repeat the process, to create a simple, two-pronged plait. Gently squeeze together the other ends so that you are left with the two intertwined halves showing the filling layers on top. Carefully lift the cake into a loaf pan. Cover the pan with a wet tea towel and leave to rise in a warm place for 2 to 2½ hours. The cake will rise by 10 to 20%. Repeat the whole process for the second cake.

8. Preheat the oven to 350°F, turning it on at least 15 minutes before the cakes have finished rising. Remove the tea towels, place the cakes on the middle rack of the oven, and bake for about 30 minutes, until a skewer inserted in the center comes out clean.

9. While the cakes are in the oven, make the syrup. Combine the water and sugar in a saucepan, place over medium heat and bring to a boil. As soon as the sugar dissolves, remove from heat and leave to cool down. As soon as the cakes come out of the oven, brush with all of the syrup. When cakes have cooled, remove from the pans and cool completely before slicing.

(turn page for step by step guide)

BABKA

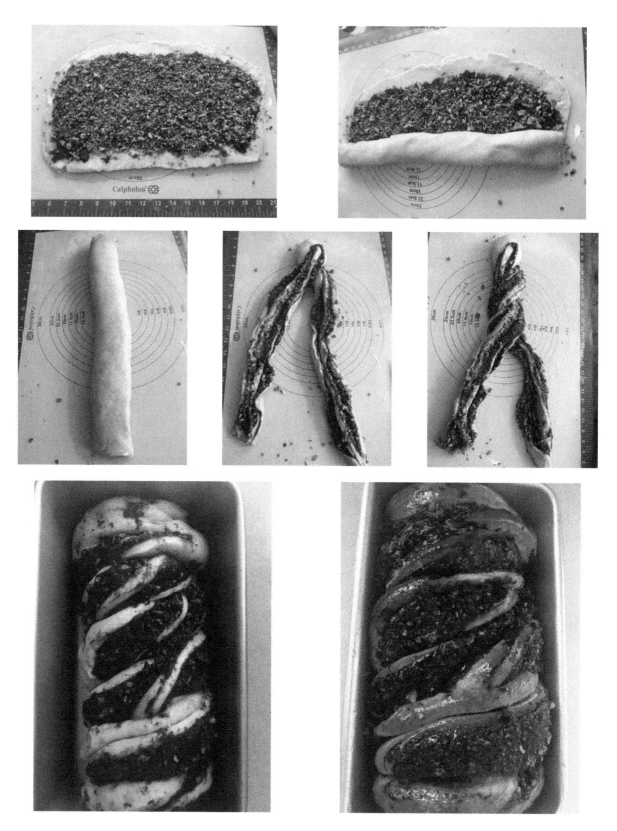

CHOCOLATE RICE PUDDING

Dairy and Gluten-free

This tastes decadent but is actually low fat, dairy and gluten free, and full of protein. Plus, isn't chocolate the new kale?

INGREDIENTS

Pudding 1 cup short grain brown rice, soaked overnight in cold water
¼ cup sugar
½ teaspoon kosher salt
2 tablespoons cocoa powder
1 vanilla bean, split and seeds scooped out
    OR 2 teaspoons vanilla extract
4½ cups almond milk

Glaze ¾ cup (125 grams) dark chocolate, roughly chopped
and ¼ cup plus 2 tablespoons strong hot coffee
Berries Fresh berries for garnish

INSTRUCTIONS

1. Combine pudding ingredients in a medium saucepan and bring to a boil. Reduce heat to very low, cover, and cook until rice is tender, 30-45 minutes. Mixture will be somewhat soupy.
2. Combine glaze ingredients and stir until chocolate melts and mixture is smooth.
3. Spoon glaze over pudding served in bowls. Garnish with fresh berries if desired.
4. Store leftovers in refrigerator, and micro-wave for 1 minute per serving or until heated as desired.

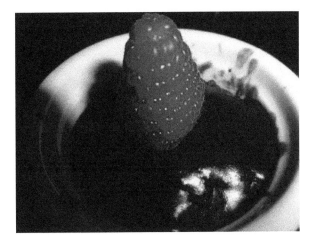

BAKLAVA

This classic Middle Eastern dessert takes some practice to really master. A delicate hand is needed to work with the sometimes temperamental filo dough. Many types of nuts work here – pecans, pistachios, walnuts and almonds – singly or in combination. This is adapted from a recipe shared by Shula Lavie.

INGREDIENTS

Filling

6 cups nuts, coarsely chopped
1 cup brown sugar
2 tablespoons Orange Flower Water
2 teaspoons ground cinnamon

Syrup

1½ cups granulated sugar
1 slice fresh ginger, peeled
3 tablespoons Orange Flower Water
2 sticks cinnamon
1¼ cups water

Dough

1 stick sweet butter, melted
   (*or* ½ cup oil for a vegan version: coconut oil *or* extra virgin olive oil *or* a combination)
1 package frozen filo dough (preferably Indo-European brand)

INSTRUCTIONS

1. Defrost the package of frozen filo dough overnight in the refrigerator.
2. Preheat the oven to 355°.
3. Prepare the syrup by putting all the *syrup* ingredients in a saucepan and bringing the mixture to a boil. Let the syrup cool completely.
4. Melt 1 stick of sweet butter in a small saucepan with a lid.
5. Chop the nut mixture in a food processor.
6. Unwrap the filo dough and cover it with a dry dish towel.
7. Lay out a sheet of the filo dough and lightly brush it with the melted butter using a large pastry brush. Repeat the process with the other 2 filo dough sheets (3 total).
8. Place some of the nut mixture along one edge of one of the sheets and then roll it into a tight roll and place the log in a buttered Pyrex dish (10" x 15").
9. Repeat the process with the rest of the sheets and place each log so that it is touching the previous one. Continue until the pan is full.
10. Cutting in diagonal lines, cut each log into 1-inch pieces. Make sure to cut all the way through. Brush the top of the logs with the remaining melted butter.
11. Bake the baklava at 355° for 1 hour, or until they are deep golden brown.
12. When the baklava is finished, spoon the cold syrup over the hot baklava and then let it cool for several hours.
13. Serve at room temperature or refrigerate for up to 2 weeks in an airtight container.

BAKLAVA

COCONUT FLAN
Dairy free

This recipe was adapted from a Vietnamese cookbook. It's like crème caramel, but dairy free.

INGREDIENTS

Caramel   ¼ cup brown sugar
           ¼ cup hot water

Custard   2 cups canned coconut milk
           ¼ cup coconut sugar
           4 eggs
           1 teaspoon vanilla extract

Syrup in the bottom   *Ready for the water*   *Sitting in the bath*   *Ready to serve*

INSTRUCTIONS

1. Preheat oven to 325°F.
2. Make caramel by cooking the brown sugar in a small heavy saucepan over low heat, swirling constantly until browned. Stir hot water into caramel slowly and continue boiling until sugar is dissolved.
3. Pour caramel into 1 quart Pyrex bowl or six 4-ounce ramekins. Tilt the molds to coat all interior surfaces with caramel.
4. To make custard, combine coconut milk and coconut sugar in a medium saucepan and cook over low heat until sugar is dissolved. Remove from heat.
5. In a large bowl, whisk eggs and vanilla. Gradually whisk in the hot mixture, blending well.
6. Pour custard into the bowl or ramekins, over the caramel.
7. Line a roasting pan with 2 layers of paper towels.
8. Place baking dish(s) in the pan and add hot water to reach halfway up the sides.
9. Bake at 325°F in center of oven for 50 minutes (30 minutes for ramekins). Test with a knife inserted in the center - it should come out clean.
10. Remove immediately from hot water and allow to cool. Chill thoroughly.
11. Serve cold. If using large glass dish, scoop out portions with a serving spoon. If using ramekins, serve in ramekin. All fruit preserves may substitute for syrup if desired.

GLUTEN FREE APPLE CRISP

This gluten free crisp started out as an apple recipe, but also can use whatever fruit is in season and at its peak, including pears, peaches, plums, apricots, cherries and/or berries. The types of fruit can be combined as you wish, with some adjustment in the amount of sweetener depending on the tartness of the fruit. Use your imagination!

INGREDIENTS

Filling

2-3 lbs fresh fruit, washed and sliced but unpeeled
2 tablespoons agave syrup or brown sugar
1 teaspoon cinnamon (only if using apples)

Topping

1½ cups gluten free oats (e.g. Bob's Redmill)
2 cups pecans, chopped
1 teaspoon cinnamon (only if using apples)
¼ cup gluten free flour
⅛ teaspoon salt
3 tablespoons butter, melted
¼ cup olive oil
½ cup maple syrup
1 teaspoon vanilla extract

INSTRUCTIONS

1. Preheat oven to 350°
2. Combine all the dry *topping* ingredients in a bowl and set aside.
3. Slice the fruit into ¼ inch slices.
4. Butter a 12" x 16" Pyrex pan and add the *filling* ingredients. Toss all *filling* ingredients into the pan.
5. Melt the butter in a small saucepan and then add the oil and maple syrup.
6. Add the dry ingredients to the oil and syrup and mix thoroughly.
7. Spoon the topping evenly over the filling in the Pyrex pan.
8. Bake the crisp for 30 – 50 minutes at 350°, until the filling is bubbling and the topping has nicely browned.
9. Serve warm or at room temperature.

HELEN ROWE'S UPSIDE DOWN LEMON PIE
Gluten-free

My mother made this as one large pie, but it is also good made as individual portions using either muffin tins or mini-muffin tins. The meringue is used to create a crust, topped with the lemon filling. The meringue is baked, and then the filling is chilled.

INGREDIENTS

Meringue
: 4 egg whites
¼ teaspoon cream of tartar
1 cup granulated sugar
Cooking oil spray for pan
  and/or paper liner(s)

Filling
: 4 egg yolks
½ cup granulated sugar
⅓ cup fresh squeezed lemon juice
Grated zest of two organic lemons
(reserve a teaspoon full for garnish
if desired)

Optional: Whipped cream, unsweetened, or coconut whipped cream (frozen)

Mini-muffin sized pies

INSTRUCTIONS

1. Preheat oven to 300ºF. Coat 10" pie pan (deep-dish) with cooking oil spray, and a paper liner in the bottom if desired. If making individual portions, use paper liners in the muffin tins and give each one a spritz of cooking oil spray.
2. Be sure to zest the lemons before squeezing the juice – it's much easier.
3. Beat egg whites until foamy, then add cream of tartar and sugar. Continue to beat until very stiff and glossy.
4. Spread egg white mixture evenly in prepared pie pan or muffin tins - across the bottom and up the sides like a crust. Bake for 1½ hours, or about 40 minutes for the individual portions. Important: Turn off heat and allow to cool for an hour in the oven. Remove pie pan or muffin tins to wire racks on the counter to finish cooling.
5. In the top of a double boiler, blend the filling ingredients well (using half the lemon zest) before placing over the boiling water in the base. Cook until thick and smooth, stirring often.
6. Allow to cool. If using whipped cream, fold in to cool filling.
7. Pour filling into meringue "crust" and sprinkle with remaining lemon zest.
8. Chill in refrigerator for 1 to 24 hours before serving.

HONEY CHIFFON CAKE
Gluten free

For years I tried a different honey cake recipe every year for Rosh Ha Shana (Jewish New Year). They were all too dry, too spicy or too heavy. When I discovered this one, my search was over!

INGREDIENTS

¾ cup honey
½ cup hot Earl Grey tea
1½ cups gluten free flour
½ teaspoon baking soda
1 heaping teaspoon baking powder
Pinch of salt
6 eggs, whites and yolks separated
¾ cup sugar
2 teaspoons vanilla extract
½ teaspoon ginger powder
1 heaping teaspoon cinnamon
¾ cup extra virgin olive oil <u>or</u> coconut oil

INSTRUCTIONS

1. Prepare two loaf pans with cooking oil spray.
2. Preheat oven to 300°F.
3. In a small bowl, combine honey and hot tea, stirring to dissolve honey.
4. Combine flour, baking soda, baking powder and salt by whisking together in a medium mixing bowl.
5. In a standing mixer, beat egg whites on high speed until frothy. Add half of the sugar and beat until stiff peaks form. Gently transfer beaten egg whites to another clean bowl and set aside. No need to wash mixer bowl before next step.
6. In the standing mixer, beat egg yolks, remaining sugar, vanilla, ginger, cinnamon and oil.
7. Add the honey mixture and the dry mixture to the egg yolk mixture in alternating batches and mix well.
8. Remove bowl from mixer stand and gently fold in the beaten egg whites.
9. Pour batter into prepared loaf pans and bake for 45 minutes to an hour, until browned and a toothpick comes out clean.
10. Remove from loaf pans and cool on wire racks. Wrap in airtight plastic when thoroughly cooled. Keep at room temperature for up to 5 days.

ISRAELI CHEESECAKE

This light and fluffy cheesecake is relatively low fat; it doesn't leave you feeling heavy.

INGREDIENTS

Crust
1 inner sleeve of Graham crackers (about 9)
4 tablespoons butter, melted
½ cup pecans

Topping
1 16-ounce tub low fat sour cream
¼ cup granulated sugar
2 teaspoons vanilla extract

Cake Filling
2 8-ounce packages Neufchatel cheese
1 cup granulated sugar
½ cup flour, regular or gluten free
1 cup low fat sour cream
2 teaspoons vanilla extract
5 large eggs, yolks and whites separated

INSTRUCTIONS

Crust
1. In a food processor, chop Graham crackers and pecans until mixture is smooth.
2. Pour the mixture into a 12 inch spring form pan.
3. Melt the butter and pour it over the crumbs.
4. Using a fork, work the butter into the crumbs. Then pat the crumb mixture by hand to evenly line the bottom of the pan and slightly up the sides.

Filling and Topping
1. Preheat oven to 325°.
2. Separate egg whites from the yolks.
3. In a standing mixer, beat the egg whites until they are stiff.
4. Remove the whites to a separate bowl and set aside. Mix the yolks with the rest of the *cake* ingredients in the mixer.
5. Continue to mix the ingredients until they are light and fluffy.
6. Fold the egg whites into the mixture by hand.
7. Pour the batter into the prepared crust and bake the cake at 325° for 1 hour.
8. While the cake is baking, combine the *topping* ingredients in a bowl and mix well.
9. Remove the cake from the oven and allow it to cool for about 15 minutes, or until it becomes flat again.
10. Pour the topping mixture over it.
11. Return the cake to the oven and bake it at 350° for another 10 minutes.
12. Cool on a rack and then cover. Refrigerate until cold and serve (min. 2 hours).

NOTE: To make dairy and/or gluten free: 2 packages dairy-free cream cheese (Tree Hill), coconut or almond yogurt instead of sour cream, and coconut oil instead of butter. Replace graham crackers with any gluten free plain cookie.

ITALIAN ALMOND COOKIES
Gluten-free

We first had these cookies on a trip to Sicily at the New Year, when bakeries were gift wrapping them for customers. I tried lots of recipes, but they were tricky to make. After many experiments, I finally got them to come out like the ones we remembered!

INGREDIENTS

1 package Almond paste (8 ounces)
Dash of salt
½ cup powdered sugar
2 egg whites
1 teaspoon almond extract
Zest of two medium lemons
½ cup Almonds, sliced thin
Powdered sugar for garnish - optional

INSTRUCTIONS

1. Heat oven to 325°F. Prepare cookie sheet with parchment or Silpat.
2. In a food processor, chop the sliced almonds using the pulse function, not too fine.
3. In a standing mixer, beat almond paste, sugar and salt until well blended.
4. Separate egg whites and yolks, setting yolks aside for another use.
5. Add egg whites to almond paste mixture to form a smooth paste.
6. Add lemon zest and almond extract and mix in well.
7. Using a small teaspoon, form balls and roll in the chopped almond slices.
8. Place balls on prepared cookie sheet, about 2" apart.
9. Bake for 16-20 minutes or until edges begin to brown, rotating cookie sheet half way through time for even baking.
10. Cool completely. Dust with powdered sugar.
11. Store in an airtight container.

LEMON ALMOND CRISPS
Gluten free

These light, flavorful cookies go well with a cup of tea or coffee - or with a scoop of vanilla ice cream!

INGREDIENTS

¼ cup fresh squeezed lemon juice
1 cup (2 sticks) unsalted butter, room temperature
2 cups gluten free all purpose flour
1 teaspoon baking powder
½ teaspoon coarse salt
1½ cups sugar
1 large egg
1 teaspoon vanilla extract
1 teaspoon lemon extract
3½ teaspoons finely grated lemon zest, divided
1 tablespoon chopped candied lemon peel
⅔ cup chopped toasted almonds

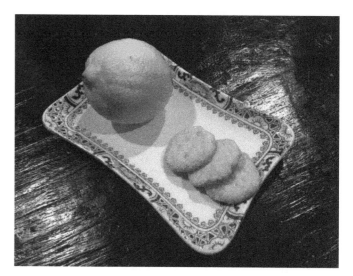

INSTRUCTIONS

1. Preheat oven to 350°F.
2. Zest the lemon before juicing it.
3. In a large bowl, whisk together flour, baking powder and salt.
4. Using an standing mixer, cream the butter with 1 cup of the sugar, using paddle attachment. Add egg, mixing until smooth and pale - about 3 minutes. Mix in extracts and 2 teaspoons of the lemon zest.
5. On low speed, gradually add flour mixture, then almonds and candied lemon peel.
6. In a small bowl, stir together remaining ½ cup of sugar and 1½ teaspoons lemon zest.
7. Form dough into 1¼ inch balls and then roll balls in the lemon zest-sugar mixture to coat.
8. On a baking sheet lined with parchment, space balls 2 inches apart. Press each with the bottom of a glass dipped in the sugar mixture. Pressed dough should be ¼ inch thick.
9. Bake until just browned around the edges, 12 to 13 minutes, rotating sheets halfway through. Allow to cool completely on the cookie sheets (placed on wire racks).
10. Cookies may be stored in an airtight container at room temperature for up to 1 week.

Note: Recipe may also be made with regular all-purpose flour.

LEMON ALMOND MUFFINS
Gluten free

My grandson Jordan is crazy about lemons. I decided to make these muffins as a healthy alternative to sweeter lemony desserts. All kids love muffins!

INGREDIENTS

I. 1½ cups almond flour/meal
    ½ cup coconut flour
    1 heaping teaspoon baking powder
    Pinch of salt

II. ½ cup coconut oil or butter
    1 cup coconut sugar
    1 teaspoon zylitol
    2 tablespoons lemon zest and juice mixture*
    3 large eggs
    1 teaspoon vanilla extract
    1 tablespoon dairy free yogurt
    1 cup fresh or frozen blueberries mixed into
       the batter (optional)

III. 6 tablespoons lemon zest and juice mixture*
        (or remaining amount from II)
     ¼ cup agave syrup

    *3 large Meyer and/or Eureka lemons, zest
       and juice combined (divided for II and III)

INSTRUCTIONS

1. Preheat oven to 325°F.
2. Prepare muffin tins - 12 standard or 24 small. Spray with cooking oil.
3. Zest the lemons before juicing them.
4. Combine section I ingredients in a bowl.
5. Combine section II oil and sugar in a mixer and blend until smooth.
6. Blend in remaining ingredients from II (except blueberries).
7. Add section I ingredients to the mixer and blend for about 1 minute.
8. Gently fold in blueberries by hand.
9. Divide batter into prepared muffin tins.
10. Bake for 20-25 minutes, until a toothpick comes out clean.
11. While muffins are baking, prepare syrup.
12. Mix section III ingredients in a bowl.
13. Brush syrup onto hot muffins, using up all the syrup.

LEMONY LEMON BARS

Over the years, I must have tried at least 20 different recipes for lemon bars. After tasting them all, I am convinced that this is the one!

INGREDIENTS

Pastry
3 ounces (¾ stick) butter
¼ cup light brown sugar
1 cup flour (regular or gluten free)

Lemon Layer
Grated rind of 4 medium lemons
½ cup fresh squeezed lemon juice
4 extra-large eggs
1½ cups granulated sugar
4 tablespoons flour (regular or gluten free)
½ teaspoon baking powder

Garnish
Powdered sugar for dusting the top

INSTRUCTIONS

Pastry
1. Preheat the oven to 350°. Adjust the rack to the center of the oven.
2. Place an 8" x 12" pan in the freezer.
3. In a food processor, place all the dry *pastry* ingredients and pulse to combine well.
4. Cut the butter in small pieces and add them to dry ingredients in the food processor. Beat until the mixture is completely smooth.
5. Grease the chilled pan and then pat the crust evenly into the bottom.
6. Bake at 350° for 15 minutes, until lightly colored.

Lemon Layer
1. In an electric mixer, beat the eggs. Add the sugar, flour and baking powder while continuing to mix.
2. Beat for 1 more minute at a high speed and then add the lemon juice and the rind.

Assembly and Baking
1. Pour the lemon mixture over the hot crust and then bake for another 25 – 30 minutes, until the top is lightly colored and dry to the touch.
2. Cool completely in the pan, dust with powdered sugar and cut into small squares.
3. Store the lemon bars in the refrigerator, in an airtight container.

MAGIC MORNING MUFFINS
Gluten-free

I was excited when a beloved local bakery here in Los Angeles shared the recipe for its popular morning muffins, but I was horrified that they were considered healthy. They were full of problematic ingredients. I set out to create a really healthy muffin that could substitute for a sit-down breakfast and this really fits the bill. Everyone loves them!!!

INGREDIENTS

Flour mixture	2 cups gluten free flour
	1 heaping teaspoon baking powder
	1 heaping teaspoon baking soda
	Pinch of salt
Wet mixture	½ cup coconut oil
	1 cup coconut sugar
	2 teaspoons zylitol
	2 teaspoons vanilla extract
	2 eggs
	2 tablespoons non-dairy yogurt
	½ cup agave syrup (or maple syrup)
Fruits, Nuts and Vegetables	1 teaspoon fresh orange zest
	1 can pumpkin (15 oz.) OR 1 large baked sweet potato, mashed
	1 teaspoon cinnamon
	1 teaspoon pumpkin pie spice blend
	1 small butternut squash, peeled and shredded (OR 2 cups shredded carrots)
	1 cup dried cranberries
	1 cup chopped pecans or dried fruit of your choice

INSTRUCTIONS

1. Preheat oven to 325°F and place paper liners in muffin tins (makes 24 regular size muffins).
2. In a medium mixing bowl, whisk flour mixture together and set aside.
3. In a standing mixer, beat together the coconut oil and sugar with the paddle attachment on medium speed for about 2 minutes. Add zylitol, vanilla, eggs, yogurt and agave syrup. Mix until well blended.
4. In a medium mixing bowl, mix together the fruits, nuts and vegetables.
5. Slowly add flour mixture to wet mixture, and beat until batter is smooth.
6. Add fruits, nuts and vegetables and mix well.
7. Spoon into prepared muffin tins.
8. Bake for 45-60 minutes, until a toothpick comes out clean.
9. Leftover muffins freeze well and reheat in a toaster oven. Wait until muffins are completely cool before packing in sealed freezer bags.

MEYER LEMON TARTS
Gluten-free

These are light, gluten free and can be dairy free, without sacrificing intense lemon flavor in a "creamy" tart.

INGREDIENTS

3 Meyer lemons, medium sized, juice without pulp, and zest
½ cup gluten free flour
Pinch of salt
¾ cup sugar
3 large eggs, separated
1 teaspoon vanilla extract
1½ cups whole milk *OR* 1 can coconut milk (15 ounce can)
Fresh fruit for topping
Whipped cream (optional)

INSTRUCTIONS

1. Preheat oven to 325°F.
2. Prepare 4 ounce individual baking dishes (6-8) with cooking oil spray. Set prepared dishes into a 9x13" baking pan.
3. Bring a kettle of water to a boil and reduce heat to lowest setting until needed.
4. Finely grate the lemon zest and then squeeze the juice. Strain out pulp.
5. In a small mixing bowl, whisk together the flour, salt and ½ cup of the sugar.
6. Separate egg whites and yolks into two small bowls.
7. In a standing mixer, beat the egg whites until they hold soft peaks, then add ¼ cup sugar and beat until stiff.
8. In a large mixing bowl, whisk together yolks, milk, lemon zest and juice, gradually adding the flour mixture.
9. Using a rubber spatula, gently fold half of the beaten egg whites into the batter, then fold in the remaining half.
10. Pour batter into prepared baking dishes.
11. Carefully pour boiling water into large pan pan until 1" up the outside of the baking dishes, taking care not to get water into the batter.
12. Bake until puffed and golden, 40 to 60 minutes.
13. Serve (in baking dishes) hot, room temperature or cold, topped with fresh fruit and whipped cream, if desired.

NOODLE KUGEL

This kugel recipe was given to me by some friends who brought it each year at the Jewish New Year celebration. It is rich, decadent and delicious. It's okay to splurge once a year...

INGREDIENTS

Noodle Mixture	1 pound wide egg noodles
	1 stick butter, cut in pieces
	1 cup whole milk
	5 large eggs, lightly beaten
	½ cup brown sugar
	2 teaspoons vanilla
	1 16-oz container sour cream
	1 16-oz container cottage cheese, 4% fat
	1 20-oz can crushed pineapple, drained
Topping	2 cups crushed corn flakes
	2 tablespoons sugar
	½ teaspoon cinnamon
	2 tablespoons butter, cut in bits

INSTRUCTIONS

1. Cook noodles until al dente. Drain, add butter and toss to coat noodles.
2. Preheat oven to 350°F.
3. Mix together other Noodle Mixture ingredients and gently combine with cooked noodles.
4. Pour into a 9x13" glass baking dish, oiled.
5. Make topping and spread evenly over kugel.
6. Bake 1 hour until golden brown.

OATMEAL CHOCOLATE CHIP LACE COOKIES

Affectionately called "Crack Cookies" at our house, these cookies are utterly addicting. Try to walk away after eating just one. Go ahead, try it...

INGREDIENTS

⅓ cup whole wheat pastry flour
¼ teaspoon salt
½ teaspoon baking soda
1¼ cups old fashioned rolled oats
1 stick butter
⅔ cup granulated sugar
⅔ cup brown sugar
1 egg
2 teaspoons vanilla extract
2 cups pecans (about 8 ounces), chopped
2 cups chocolate chips

INSTRUCTIONS

1. Preheat the oven to 350°.
2. Mix the flour, salt, baking soda and oats in a bowl and then set aside.
3. In a mixer, cream the butter with both of the sugars until fluffy. Add the egg and vanilla. Continue to combine the ingredients until they are well mixed.
4. Add the flour mixture and the chopped nuts to the creamed ingredients. Continue mixing.
5. Add the chocolate chips and continue mixing.
6. Form the batter into balls with a ½" diameter.
7. Line 2 cookie sheets with silpat and place the balls on the sheets.
8. Bake the cookies for 10 – 20 minutes, or until they are brown and lacy.
9. Remove from the oven and set to cool.
10. Once they are cooled, remove them from the sheets and store in airtight containers.
11. Cookies will keep for up to 2 weeks.

For a gluten free version: use gluten free flour and oats, increase baking soda to 1 teaspoon. Bake at 325°.

RUGALACH THINS

These tasty thin cookies are a twist on classic rugalach, and provide slice-and-bake convenience.

INGREDIENTS

Filling

2 cups pecans
¾ cup raisins
⅔ cup brown sugar
2 teaspoons cinnamon
4 tablespoons butter, cut in 4 pieces
1 teaspoon vanilla extract
grated peel of 1 organic lemon

Dough

4 egg yolks <u>or</u> 2 whole eggs
2 sticks butter
1 teaspoon vanilla extract
1½ teaspoons baking powder
juice of 1 orange
grated peel of ½ organic orange
1½ cups sugar
3 cups white unbleached flour
1 cup whole wheat pastry flour

INSTRUCTIONS

1. In a food processor, combine the filling ingredients (pecans, raisins, brown sugar, cinnamon, butter, vanilla and grated lemon peel) and pulse to chop nuts and combine.
2. In a mixer, combine the dough ingredients (eggs, butter, vanilla extract, baking powder, orange juice, orange peel, sugar and flour). Mix on a slow setting.
3. Divide the dough and the filling into 6 equal parts. Roll out into rectangles and spread filling on dough, leaving a half inch bare at the end of the dough.
4. Roll the dough into a log about 1 inch in diameter, sealing it with the bare margin. Repeat.
5. Wrap each log with plastic wrap and seal the wrap by tucking the edges under the ends.
6. Place the wrapped logs in the freezer for a minimum of 2 hours. The frozen dough can be kept in the freezer for months and used as needed.
7. Preheat the oven to 350°.
8. Remove the dough logs from the freezer and then slice the logs thinly.
9. Place the wafer-thin slices on a silpat and bake them for 11 minutes at 350°.
10. Allow the cookies to cool and then serve.
11. Baked cookies will keep in an airtight container for up to 1 week.

SABA'S SWEET SAMBUSAK
Dessert Turnovers

My sainted father in law, Saba Itzhak, taught me how to make these delicacies. Like many other Iraqi Jewish desserts, they aren't overly sweet and are a great accompaniment to a cup of coffee or tea. On his visits to the US, Saba would sit in our kitchen and make hundreds of them to be frozen in plastic bags. We always think of him when we make them now. I pop them into the toaster oven to warm before serving, and they taste freshly baked. You can safely freeze them for 6 months....if they last that long! (Chickpea Sambusak, p. 10, uses the same process)

INGREDIENTS

Filling
2 cups finely chopped pecans
¾ cup brown sugar
1 teaspoon cardamom
½ teaspoon cinnamon
2 tablespoons butter
  (or dairy free substitute)

Dough
2 cups white flour
1¾ cups whole wheat pastry flour
  (or white whole wheat flour)
¼ cup extra virgin olive oil (or canola or avocado)
½ teaspoon salt
½ package yeast
4 tablespoons sugar
Warm water, as needed

INSTRUCTIONS

Filling
1. Finely chop pecans and combine with sugar and spices in a bowl. Set aside.

Dough
1. Dissolve yeast in ½ cup of warm water with ½ teaspoon of sugar to proof.
2. Put all the other dough ingredients into a bowl and add the proofed yeast mixture.
3. Knead dough until smooth. The dough should be firm, not sticky. Add additional water as needed to achieve smooth consistency.
4. Place dough in an oiled bowl, turn over to coat all sides, cover with a dish towel and let rise for 1 hour.

Assembly and Baking
1. Preheat oven to 350°F
2. Roll out ¼ of the dough until it is about ⅛ of an inch thick.
3. Cut circles in the dough with a cookie cutter or jelly glass.
4. Place 1 heaping teaspoon of the filling into the middle of each dough circle and pinch closed to make half moon shapes.
5. Bake at 350° on cookie sheets, about 15 – 20 minutes, until golden brown.
6. Repeat the process with the rest of the dough and filling.
7. Thoroughly cooled sambusak can be frozen in freezer bags until needed. Simply reheat in a 400° toaster oven until heated through.

COMPLETE RECIPE LISTING IN ALPHABETICAL ORDER

COMPLETE RECIPE LISTING IN ALPHABETICAL ORDER

NOTES AND REMINDERS

Andrea Tzadik has lived in New York, California, Israel, Iowa, Connecticut and California – in that order. She has collected and refined recipes from all these locations plus travel adventures, cooking with enthusiasm for her family and friends while working in real estate and raising four children.

CPSIA information can be obtained
at www.ICGtesting.com
Printed in the USA
BVHW02*2029070918

526517BV00005B/3/P